BEGINNING AGAIN

D. James Kennedy, Ph.D.

with

Norman R. Wise

tCRmPublishing

Ft. Lauderdale, FL

Table of Contents

Letter From Dr. Kennedy
How To Use This Book

Part One: Beginning With Him

Part Two: The Gospel of John

Part Three: Other Helps for Beginning Again

Dear Friend:

This booklet has been written to help those who have recently asked Jesus Christ to be their Lord and Savior. Its purpose is to assist new believers to grow in their understanding of His will for their lives.

When we trust in Christ we begin a lifelong relationship with the greatest Friend we will ever know. It is important that we nourish this relationship with Jesus so that it has the greatest possible impact on our lives.

It is a sad fact that I have met hundreds of people who **suppose** that they can **earn** their way into Heaven by becoming church members or by living a moral life, rather than having a personal relationship with Christ. These things are certainly commendable, but they can in no way obtain eternal life in Heaven with God.

The Bible tells us in Romans 6:23, **"For the wages of sin is death, but the gift of God is eternal life in Christ our Lord."** Heaven is a gift! We need only reach out and take Jesus as our personal Savior and Lord and Heaven is ours.

The reason for this is that God's standard for Heaven is **perfection,** yet no one has ever lived a perfect life, except Jesus Christ. Sin separates us from God. The good deeds we may do can never overcome this gap or earn for us God's blessing. Left on our own, we are lost and without any hope of eternal life in Heaven.

However, God solved this dilemma for us through Jesus (John 1:1,14; James 2:10). Jesus, who is God in the flesh, loved us so much that He left His glorious home to live in our sin-sick world. He took abuse, suffering and death in our place, paying God's penalty for sin on the cross.

They placed His body in a tomb and sealed it. **Yet, He did not remain in the grave, but rose from the dead.** He is now in Heaven preparing a place for all those who trust in Him alone for their salvation.

Jesus is the **only** way to Heaven. The Scriptures teach us, "**. . . Believe in the Lord Jesus Christ, and you shall be saved . . . " (Acts 16:31).** It is made clear in this passage that we must welcome Jesus into our lives as **Lord** and **Savior.** To accept Jesus as LORD means to accept Him as the Ruler and King of our lives. To **receive Him as Savior** is to depend solely on His death on the cross to pay for our sins.

To truly believe means we must repent of our sins and trust in Jesus to save us from the punishment of Hell. God has promised that all who do this will be granted the joy of Heaven (John 3:16; 14:6). Jesus promises that when we accept Him into our lives He will be with us now and forever.

Once we know Jesus as our personal Lord and Savior, our "thank you" to Him for the suffering He endured for us will be to serve Him in every area of our life. To do this we will need to attend church to worship God and study the Scripture. This will help us to get to know Him better and thus learn how we can live in a way that pleases Him.

May God guide you in your new life in Christ. It is my prayer that this booklet will help every reader to better understand what the abundant life with Christ is all about and how you can realize His richest blessings.

In His service,

D. James Kennedy

HOW TO USE THIS BOOK!

1. Read each of the chapters carefully and answer the questions at the end. Check your answers by referring to the answers in the back of the book, beginning with page 125.

2. Read one chapter of John each day for the next 21 days.

3. Before you read the Gospel of John, review "Getting Into the Bible" on page 24, where Dr. Kennedy explains how to understand the Bible.

4. Read the Introduction and the Outline preceding the first chapter of the Gospel of John. Taking this initial step will enhance your understanding.

5. Take special note of the words in **bold print.** Any word that has been placed in bold print is of special importance.

6. Helpful hints are given on page 123 on choosing a church. A form you can fill out and mail to us is also included if you would like to contact us for a reference of a Bible-believing church in your area.

7. A list of memory verses is included. Cutting these verses out and carrying them with you so that you can review them occasionally will greatly aid memorization. Generally, it is advisable to only attempt to memorize one verse per week.

PART ONE

Beginning With Him

Chapter 1

YOU ARE GOING TO HEAVEN!

You have made the most important decision anyone can make! You have decided to receive Jesus Christ as your own Lord and Savior and have begun a new and exciting adventure.

But there are many things you now need to know and learn. One of the first things is to be *absolutely certain* of your final destination; to know for certain that you are on your way to Heaven.

The Bible teaches that we *can know* we have eternal life in Heaven! The Apostle John writes:

I write these things to you who believe in the name of the Son of God so that you may know that you have eternal life.

(1 John 5:13)

Isn't that a tremendous proclamation? The promise of God is that all who sincerely and truly believe in Jesus Christ can know that they have been granted eternal life in Heaven as a free gift.

Even the most casual reading of the New Testament will reveal that one of the most striking characteristics of the Apostles and the entire Apostolic Church was this element of certainty.

These were men who **knew**. They didn't hope; they didn't wish — they **knew**! They knew their sins were forgiven; they knew they had received eternal life. They knew beyond all doubt that they were on their way to Heaven.

Today, many find this to be the most startling fact found in the New Testament. And yet, we read that the Apostles said:

WE KNOW THAT WE HAVE PASSED FROM DEATH TO LIFE, because we love our brothers. Anyone who does not love remains in death (1 John 3:14).

WE KNOW THAT WE ARE CHILDREN OF GOD, and that the whole world is under the control of the evil one (1 John 5:19).

IN HIM WE HAVE REDEMPTION THROUGH HIS BLOOD, THE FORGIVENESS OF SINS, in accordance with the riches of God's grace . . . (Ephesians 1:7).

Dear friends, **NOW WE ARE CHILDREN OF GOD** and what we will be has not yet been made known. **BUT WE KNOW THAT WHEN HE APPEARS, WE SHALL BE LIKE HIM,** for we shall see Him as He is (1 John 3:2).

. . . **Neither height nor depth, nor anything else in all creation, will be able to separate us from the love of God that is in Christ Jesus our Lord** (Romans 8:39).

We know that we know! Affirmation is piled on top of affirmation. The Apostles not only knew, but they knew that they knew!

It was this certainty, this unshakable faith, that enabled the Apostles to withstand every difficulty, to overcome every obstacle, and to turn the world right side up for Jesus Christ. This was no mere vain boast, but rather a ringing, glorious affirmation of faith in Jesus Christ; a stirring testimony to the risen Lord Jesus.

I, D. James Kennedy, am going to Heaven. But it's not because of what I've done or because of what I am. It's because of what Christ did for me. I'm going to Heaven not because of what I am, but **in spite** of what I am.

Salvation is a free gift, and you can't boast about a gift. You can only be thankful. It is no achievement of mine. It is not because I think I am good or pious or holy, because I know I am none of these. I know that I am sinful and wicked and belong in Hell. But I am going to Heaven!

That is the Gospel, the Good News of Jesus Christ. This message of God's love is summarized in the following passages which we all need to think about every day:

> **For God so loved the world that he gave his one and only Son, that whoever believes in him shall not perish but have eternal life.**

> **(John 3:16)**

> **For it is by grace you have been saved, through faith — and this not from yourselves, it is the gift of GOD — NOT BY WORKS, SO THAT NO ONE CAN BOAST.**

> **(Ephesians 2:8,9)**

These passages teach clearly that eternal life is through Jesus and that one is not saved from divine punishment for their sins through doing good works, but only by Jesus . . . through faith. If you truly believe in Jesus Christ, then you can know you have been forgiven, and made God's child.

Do you take God at His Word? God has promised that if you trust in Christ, He has made you a new creature

13

(2 Corinthians 5:17), and with Fanny Crosby, the blind hymnist, you can sing "Blessed assurance, Jesus is mine."

As you begin your day with God, may I encourage you to spend a little time reading the Gospel of John found in this book. Also, thank God in prayer for the salvation He has given you. Each day we need to rejoice in the "amazing grace" which God has given us through Jesus.

TEST YOURSELF ON CHAPTER 1

1. What was a striking characteristic of the Apostolic Church?

    _____

    _____

    _____

2. How was this characteristic helpful in establishing the early Church?

    _____

    _____

    _____

3. Can we know for sure that we have eternal life? How?

    _____

    _____

    _____

4. List some verses from Scripture which confirm your answer.

    _____

    _____

    _____

Chapter 2

STAYING RIGHT WITH GOD

The first day of your new life with Jesus Christ is the greatest day of your life! It is the day in which your sins are forgiven and that you are on your way to Heaven.

We have seen how to get right with God through trusting Christ. Now we want to consider how you can **stay** right with God, day after day and year after year. Our text for this study is Colossians 2:6,7, where we read:

> **So then, just as you received Christ Jesus as Lord, continue to live in him, rooted and built up in him, strengthened in the faith as you were taught, and overflowing with thankfulness.**

This verse teaches us that we are to walk each day in faith and be full of thankfulness for God's merciful salvation.

It is unfortunate that in many cases, not long after beginning the Christian life, the joy is dissolved and the experience of the presence of God is no longer felt. Even the assurance is diminished. It is puzzling and frustrating to the new Christian and they do not know what to do because they do not understand what is happening to them.

One of the reasons for the loss of joy may be that sin has overtaken their lives; it has hidden the face of God from them, and it has robbed them of their initial joy and peace. Many feel themselves forsaken by God and some completely despair of feeling that joy of God's fellowship again.

We need to understand what God would have us do regarding this matter of sin in our lives. Perhaps you are one who would pray with King David,

Restore to me the joy of your salvation and grant me a willing spirit, to sustain me.

(Psalm 51:12)

The answer to such a spiritual problem is found in the text which I quoted earlier, Colossians 2:6,7. This passage is vital for an effective spiritual life. Hide this verse in your heart and write it upon the walls of your mind.

This is God's secret for walking in the Christian life; of not only getting right with God, but also of **staying** right with Him. This verse clearly teaches that, just as we became a Christian through faith in Christ, we must walk each day by faith.

Chosen in Spite of Ourselves

If you are a child of God — and I trust that in sincerity you have turned your life over to Christ — then you were chosen as such **in spite of what you are**, not because of what you are.

God knew from all eternity everything that you were and everything that you would be. When God redeemed you, He did not choose you because of any goodness that He saw in you. Therefore, He also does not keep you because of any goodness in you.

Is this not also true in our human relationships? You do not love your children because they are good, because they are clean, or because they are well-dressed. No, to the contrary, you do all in your power to make them well-behaved, well-dressed, well-mannered and clean, *because* you love them. You do not love them because they are bathed; you bathe them because you love them.

This is what is taught in God's Word. And this teaching can change your life if you will realize that, just as you are, God — for Christ's sake — receives you. Just as we are, without anything to commend us outside the Lord Jesus Christ, is how each of us must come before God.

Does this minimize sin? Not in the least! Sin was fully dealt with on the cross. There, between Heaven and Hell, the Son of God endured in His own body and soul the wrath that our sins deserve. God does not blink at sin or ignore it. God dealt with it fully in His Son who received and endured an infinite punishment in our stead. Therefore, we need to know that God loves us just as we are, and for Christ's sake, accepts us. By His grace He is making us what He would have us to be — more like Jesus.

God Holds You and Will Not Let Go

If you know that you are a Christian — if you know that you are going to Heaven and if you know that you are God's child — then you know that God accepted you just as you were the moment you trusted in Christ. But since that time, perhaps you have returned to your own works, trusting that they will make you acceptable to God. Now you may fear coming to Him because you do not believe that you are still acceptable.

My friend, **you never were and you never will be acceptable to God in your own right.** Yet, in Christ, we are accepted even though we are entirely unacceptable; beloved though unlovely.

Many Christians (especially new ones) when they sin feel, "Oh, how could this be? How could I have done this against God who has done so much for me? I suppose I'm not even a Christian anymore." They are afraid to come into God's presence. They turn away from His Word and from prayer — the very thing the devil desires them to do.

What should they do? They should go immediately to a gracious Father who loves them, knowing that He will receive them, and in the name of Christ, confess their sins and claim anew His forgiveness and refilling with His Spirit. We live the Christian life by constantly confessing and repenting of our sins, and by faith claiming and taking hold of the grace of God and His forgiveness in Christ.

By doing this, I believe we will find that we can live our lives far more righteously than we have previously. This does not mean that we will never sin, but it does mean that when we do sin, we are not going to get into that downward spiral which takes us even farther away from God.

Remember, God has promised to receive us when we live each day in the attitude described in 1 John 1:8-10:

If we claim to be without sin, we deceive ourselves and the truth is not in us. If we confess our sins, he is faithful and just and will forgive us our sins and purify us from all unrighteousness. If we claim we have not sinned, we make him out to be a liar and his word has no place in our lives.

This verse outlines the walk of faith that we are to have each moment of each day. The Christian clearly, moment by moment, should acknowledge his sin and depend solely on Jesus for his acceptance by God.

The Dual Nature

Many Christians cannot understand why they do the things they do. Perhaps they need to learn and understand more clearly the great truth of what happened to them when they became Christians.

What did happen? The Bible teaches that when Christ comes into our hearts, He creates a new life — a new nature within us. But this new nature does not obliterate the old. The Christian, therefore, is a unique individual in whom two natures dwell — the old nature and the new.

The old nature does not have the ability to do good! That is why before one is regenerated by God he can do nothing but sin. The reason for this is because our motives for everything we do before regeneration are wrong. We are self-centered rather than God-centered. On the other hand, the new nature cannot sin at all.

The battle waged between these two natures is described by the Apostle Paul in the following words:

> **For the sinful nature desires what is contrary to the Spirit, and the Spirit what is contrary to the sinful nature. They are in conflict with each other, so that you do not do what you want.**

> **(Galatians 5:17)**

Now the question is: to which nature are we going to yield ourselves? In the book of Romans, Paul gives his first instruction to the believer concerning how to deal with this inner battle. He says:

> **Do not offer the parts of your body to sin, as instruments of wickedness, but rather offer yourselves to God, as those who have been brought from death to life; and offer the parts of your body to him as instruments of righteousness.**

> **(Romans 6:13)**

The secret of the successful Christian life is letting the new nature control our lives. (This has also been described as having Christ on the throne of our lives.) When the new nature is "plugged in," so to speak, our life is going to bring forth the fruit of the Spirit.

But the fruit of the Spirit is love, joy, peace, patience, kindness, goodness, faithfulness, gentleness, and self-control. Against such things there is no law.

(Galatians 5:22,23)

When we bear the fruit of the Holy Spirit, we live lives pleasing to God and consistent with our confession of faith in Jesus as our Lord and Savior.

When the old nature is "plugged in," there are all kinds of works of the flesh which are difficult to live with: strife, jealousy, animosity, hatred, lust, covetousness and greed (Galatians 5:19-21). When we produce such works we are not pleasing to God and are failing to demonstrate evidence of the faith in our lives. If our entire lifestyle is controlled by such attitudes, we must question if we have sincerely trusted in Christ as the Lord of our lives.

How about you? Which nature is going to control your life? Go to God in prayer and to His Word. Pray daily that Christ will control your life. This can make each day a great adventure with God.

Try this today: As soon as you are aware of any sin in your life — any tone of voice, any look in your eye, any attitude of your heart that is not pleasing to God — then recognize that your old nature is asserting itself. Confess the sin and ask to be controlled by the Spirit of God. Ask for His mercy and His forgiveness.

What a difference it will make in your day, and you will begin to make Jesus Christ known to others through your lifestyle. God desires to see this manifestation of Christ demonstrated in our daily attitudes, words and conduct.

TEST YOURSELF ON CHAPTER 2

1. After we become children of God by accepting Christ, what does He command us to do from then on?

   _____

   _____

   _____

2. What is one of the reasons Christians lose the joy of their salvation?

   _____

   _____

   _____

3. What should a Christian do when he realizes this?

   _____

   _____

   _____

4. What makes us acceptable to God?

   _____

   _____

   _____

5. Can we choose between the old and new natures?

   _____

   _____

   _____

6. How can we keep the old nature from asserting itself?

   _____

   _____

   _____

Chapter 3

GETTING INTO THE BIBLE

There are two important aspects of the Bible; first, what it teaches concerning itself, and second, how we can go about studying it more effectively. It is vital that every new Christian clearly understand these two aspects.

All Scripture Is From God

Let's begin with what the Bible teaches concerning itself. Does the Scripture claim that it is inspired?

All Scripture is God-breathed and is useful for teaching, rebuking, correcting and training in righteousness, so that the man of God may be thoroughly equipped for every good work.

(2 Timothy 3:16,17)

Note that it says, **"ALL SCRIPTURE IS GOD-BREATHED."** In this verse the Bible claims to be inspired, and it says that this inspiration is *plenary*. That is, all Scripture (the totality of Scripture) is inspired by God. This means not just part of it, but **ALL** of it.

This, therefore, does not allow one to exclude, cafeteria style, those particular parts of the Bible that do not suit one's taste. The inspiration of Scripture includes, for example, the creation stories of Genesis, as well as the miracle stories of the Gospels, the virgin birth, Jonah and his great fish, and Noah and the Flood.

I mention these as some of the portions which skeptics and unbelievers are most likely to attack and deny. But, if all Scripture is given by inspiration of God, then it is either all inspired or it is not inspired. **The Bible's claim is that all Scripture is given from God.**

We should note that if the Bible is inspired by God, then it will be true. ". . . **YOUR WORD IS TRUTH,**" says Christ to His Father (John 17:17). The Lord of Glory, Jesus Christ, says — **"THE SCRIPTURE CANNOT BE BROKEN . . ."** (John 10:35). Jesus taught that the Scriptures are infallible and true in all their parts.

All the statements of the Bible, all of its promises, all of its prophecies, all of its declarations are true because they are inspired by the God of truth. We believe, as Christians, and the historic Orthodox Christian faith has always believed, that the Bible is **plenarily, verbally** and **infallibly** inspired. This means that **all** of the Scriptures, not only the ideas but also the words, are inspired in such a way that the Bible cannot err.

Scripture Is the Very Breath of God

According to the Bible, Scripture is the very breath of God:

> Then say to Pharaoh, *"This is what the Lord says:* Israel is my firstborn son . . ."
>
> **(Exodus 4:22)**

> Before David got up the next morning, *the word of the Lord* had come to Gad the prophet, David's seer . . .
>
> **(2 Samuel 24:11)**

> Elisha said, *"Hear the word of the Lord. This is what the Lord says:* About this time tomorrow, a seah of flour will sell for a shekel and two seahs of barley for a shekel at the gate of Samaria."
>
> **(2 Kings 7:1)**

Throughout Scripture, from Genesis to Revelation, there is this pervasive fact . . . God speaks to man.

The Bible VERIFIES its claim of inspiration and even tells us how we can do so. You don't have to devise means of discovering whether this frequently repeated claim of inspiration is true or not. God tells you the way to find out.

God says that we can know if a prophet has been sent by Him because he prophesies the future, and it comes to pass 100% of the time.

> **But the prophet who prophesies peace will be recognized as one truly sent by the Lord only if his prediction comes true.**

> **(Jeremiah 28:9)**

This declaration is not to be understood to mean a few isolated prophecies which are partly right and partly wrong. Anybody can guess and guess right part of the time, but the Bible claims a vast number of prophecies which infallibly have come to pass.

Christ: The Fulfillment of Prophecy

These prophecies concern the very center of the teaching of the Bible — the main personage about whom the Scriptures were written. That Person, of course, is Jesus of Nazareth, the Messiah of God, the Savior of the world. Here the amazing wisdom of God is seen.

One of the great functions of the Old Testament was to promise that a Messiah was to come in the fullness of time to redeem mankind. But how could the Messiah be identified?

The identification would be done in this way: various facets of His life would be prophesied forming a picture of the Messiah. Then, when He came, the picture could be put together and He could be identified. The prophecies are like the pieces of a jigsaw puzzle, except that each piece contains a complete event, not just the portion of one.

In themselves, the individual prophesies may not seem to mean much, but when you put them all together, they form a perfect picture. The Old Testament contains scores of prophecies concerning the coming of a Savior.

No other book in the world even purports to have 100% fulfilled prophecies. When the scores of tiny pieces of prophecy are fitted together, a perfect mosaic is formed that describes and pictures Jesus Christ so intimately, so perfectly, that those who have carefully examined it cannot help but be impressed by it. (See a list of some of the prophecies on pages 120-121.)

This is not the only reason that Christians believe the Bible to be true, but it is one of the most important. When the Bible is carefully and rationally examined, it proves to be more than merely a human book about religion, but rather an inspired document which is the Word of God.

The Bible Is Your Spiritual Lifeblood — Study It Carefully

Having seen something of the inspiration and nature of Scripture, let us now consider how to study the Word of God. We need to remember that this Book is different from any other book written in this world. It is the living, quickening, life-giving Word of God.

As we study the Bible, we need to remember the following words of the Apostle Peter:

Like newborn babies, crave pure spiritual milk, so that by it you may grow up in your salvation . . .

(1 Peter 2:2)

We are to study the Bible. We are to meditate upon it. We are to hide it in our hearts, to memorize it. Then God will use it to transform our lives.

There are various types of reading in the Bible. It's not simply a book; it's a whole library! But for the moment, it is probably best if you confine yourself to the New Testament — particularly to the Gospel of John.

It is important to set aside a certain time each day to study the Scriptures. Many feel that this special time should be in the morning, so that God can use it to bless your whole day.

As you select the passage to read, you should come to it expectantly, believing and praying that God the Holy Spirit will enlighten your mind and bring understanding for receiving the Word He has for you. Remember that you are coming to the Word of the living God; to a God who delights to bless your life, who has something for you every day and who wants to speak to you. God speaks to us through His Word, and we speak to Him through prayer.

Now, after you read a portion of Scripture — a few verses or a chapter — it's good to develop the habit of observation by really looking at what you have read. Too often people read through a passage and then get up and go away, hardly knowing what they have read.

Try to observe. You will find it a helpful habit to keep a notebook and to indicate what chapter of Scripture you have read and what you have observed. As you carefully read the Scriptures, you are going over ground which is tremendously wealthy — ground in which is buried all sorts of precious gems of truth. **Read and note carefully what you read.**

Take Steps To Interpret Your Scripture Passage

After you have observed as much as you can about the text, the second thing to do is to interpret what the Scripture says. Every person is responsible for interpreting the Bible. There are, however, some basic interpretive principles that you should follow.

1. **The Bible is its own interpreter.** Difficult passages are often explained in their context. A text without a context is a pretext. Some people say that the Bible can be made to say anything you want it to say. This is true only if you ignore this principle.

   First of all, when we are reading Scripture we need to ask ourselves, what does the author of this text mean to say? Always look at the text very carefully and do not come to a hasty conclusion as to what it says.

   For example, how many times have you heard it stated, "The Bible teaches that money is the root of all evil"? There are many people who would swear the Bible says this. Yet what it actually says is, "THE **LOVE** OF MONEY IS THE ROOT OF ALL KINDS OF EVIL" (1 Timothy 6:10). There is quite a difference in the meaning.

   The immediate context helps to shed light on the meaning of the text; to see the jewel in its setting where God has placed it, so that we might better understand what the text really means.

2. **We must study the text as it relates to the whole analogy of Scripture** (that is the total context of the

29

entire Bible). To repeat, the Bible explains itself, and if something is obscure in one place, there will be other places where it speaks more clearly.

Therefore, you should learn to use a concordance to look up different passages in the Bible. After comparing the text you are studying with others and interpreting it as best you can on your own, it would be well to get a good commentary to help you interpret the Scripture further.

3. **Apply what you read.** We're not simply to read Scripture, then go our own way and forget it. We are to apply it to ourselves. But what does this mean? It means that there are certain things you might want to underline. And don't be afraid to mark your Bible. Some people use colored pencils or make notes in the margin so that their Bibles will be more helpful to them.

If we follow these simple rules of Bible study, we will be able to read the Bible and learn for ourselves the truth of God and His will for our lives.

Here's What To Look For

One thing you should look for while reading the Scriptures is a **promise from God.** It's a good practice to learn the promises of God. It has been stated that our whole life, at its conclusion, will be seen simply as an unfolding of God's fulfillment of the promises He has made.

Yet, many of us fail to live our lives to the fullest because we do not claim the promises God has made to us. They are like uncashed checks. They are there for our taking, but we need to learn them; we need to claim them by faith, to trust God for them.

You have trusted Christ for your eternal salvation, and He has assured you He will take you to be with Him in Heaven. Now you can learn the joy of trusting Him for temporal things as well — for the material things and for every other aspect of your life. God is concerned with even the smallest details of our lives.

You need to learn to trust Him for your family, your business, your finances — for every decision and every need. Learn to rest upon Him. Learn the secret of spiritual serenity — and this you will learn, in part, by learning to rely on the promises of God.

There may also be a **commandment** in the passage for you to obey. This is something that is important for you to heed and obey. If you truly love Christ, you will want to keep His commandments (John 14:21). As you do, you will realize that He is wise and loving and that His commandments are not burdensome, but are given simply to make our lives the richest and the fullest possible.

Finally, there may be some **example** for you to follow or avoid. The Scriptures are filled with examples — some bad, some good — but they are examples from which you can learn. Godly men and women can be found in the Scriptures whose examples can be an encouragement and inspiration to you. The history of ungodly men and women are there as a warning not to do as they did.

All of these things will help your daily time of Scripture reading, study and meditation to be one of rich blessing and fulfillment in your life, rather than a duty to perform. I trust that as you read the Word of God today and throughout the rest of your life, God will make it a continuing and more exciting adventure with Him.

TEST YOURSELF ON CHAPTER 3

1. What are the two main aspects of the Bible which are important to you as a Christian?

   _____

   _____

   _____

2. Does the Bible claim to be inspired? List a verse to support your answer.

   _____

   _____

   _____

3. Define the following:

   a. Plenarily inspired

      _____

      _____

      _____

   b. Infallibly inspired

      _____

      _____

      _____

4. Scripture is the very breath of God. What does this mean?

_____

_____

_____

5. Retrace the steps of careful Scripture study.

_____

_____

_____

6. List the steps of Scripture interpretation.

_____

_____

_____

Chapter 4

PRACTICING THE ART OF PRAYER

We have considered the importance of Scripture and how God speaks to man. Now I would like us to consider the other half of that dialogue — how we speak to God.

We will center our discussion of this subject around James 1:2-8, which reads:

> **Consider it pure joy, my brothers, whenever you face trials of many kinds, because you know that the testing of your faith develops perseverance. Perseverance must finish its work so that you may be mature and complete, not lacking anything. If any of you lacks wisdom, he should ask God, who gives generously to all without finding fault, and it will be given to him. But when he asks, he must believe and not doubt, because he who doubts is like a wave of the sea, blown and tossed by the wind. That man should not think he will receive anything from the Lord; he is a double-minded man, unstable in all he does.**

This passage points out our need to recognize God's use of difficulties in our lives in order to develop character in our souls. It also points to believing prayer as the proper response to such trials.

The divine art of prayer is a personal linkage with the Eternal. It is communion with power unseen which transforms lives in ways that are absolutely unaccountable by those who reject belief in God.

The greatest of God's men and women have always been men and women who have learned the art of prayer. Our great exemplar, the Son of God Himself, was preeminently a man of prayer. He often rose up long before daylight and went out alone onto a mountain to pray.

I believe one of the greatest reasons for the rise of mental illness in this nation today is the lack of personal prayer. I say this without fear of contradiction, for the Scripture says:

> **Do not be anxious about anything, but in everything, by prayer and petition, with thanksgiving, present your requests to God. And the peace of God, which transcends all understanding, will guard your hearts and your minds in Christ Jesus.**
>
> **(Philippians 4:6,7)**

If our requests with thanksgiving are not made, and our eyes are not fixed upon the Christ of perfect peace, then our hearts indeed will be filled with anxiety and they will be torn this way and that.

How Do We Pray?

". . . LORD, TEACH US TO PRAY . . ." (Luke 11:1) was the heart cry of the disciples as they looked at Him who lived in perfect communion with the living God. We also need to seek God's guidance on how to pray.

Listed below are some of the basic elements of prayer which God has revealed in His Word:

1. <u>Confession</u>

   Prayer consists of certain basic elements. Unquestionably, one of these is confession. God is holy, therefore we need to place all of our sins under the blood of Christ (1 John 1:8,9).

   Any genuine understanding of God and ourselves will require that we approach Him with the confession of our sins and a sense of being totally unworthy to come into His presence. Furthermore, we must not be satisfied with a *general* confession of our sins but should also confess and repent of *particular* sins.

2. Thanksgiving

Second, there is the element of thanksgiving — thanking God for all that He has done for us. This changes the attitude of the soul from sour to sweet. What a blessing it is to see a holy contentment with our lot in life.

There is a sense in which we should have a holy discontentment, but that should be with our own spiritual progress and not with God.

Have you recently praised God for all the gifts and mercy He has poured out on your life? It is good for us to count our blessings and give all the praise to God alone for our success.

3. Petition

A third element in prayer is petition. We are to ask God for things which will help us serve Him better and provide for the needs of His people. If we have made progress in prayer, we will find these petitions will have to do primarily with our spiritual growth and not with selfish desires.

It is not wrong to bring physical needs to God in prayer, as He is concerned for the very hairs upon our heads (Matthew 10:30). However, as progress is made in the school of prayer, we will concern ourselves more with other things. We will also come to realize that our Father in Heaven knows WE HAVE NEED OF THESE THINGS (Luke 12:30).

4. Intercession

A fourth element is intercession. As we move into the "college level" of prayer, we begin to pray for other people. The needs of this world are vast. Jesus is the Great Intercessor. Paul was a great intercessor. Often, even when in prison, Paul prayed for others.

Pray for your minister. Pray for those who have authority over you. Pray for our world, and pray for lost people with whom you rub shoulders each day. There may be some in your family who do not yet know Christ. You should pray each day for them that they will come to discover what you have discovered.

5. Adoration

The fifth element of prayer is adoration — sometimes the least exercised form of prayer. This is not merely thanking God for what He has given us, but praising Him for what He is. Yet, little of our prayers consist of adoration.

Prayer Requirements for the Christian

The Bible also lays down certain conditions for prayer. If we come to God and ask for something, we should first see what God has said about the kind of prayers He will hear and answer.

1. A Right Relationship With God

First of all, the Bible requires a right relationship with God before we can expect that our prayers will be answered. This means we must be saved and not lost. We must be His children and not the children of the devil. We must be adopted into the family of God — born again into His family.

We must be regenerated, justified, repentant of our sins and by faith have received Jesus Christ into our hearts. Then, and only then, can we enter into a right relationship with God. Otherwise, the Bible says we are at enmity with God; we are outlaws and rebels against Heaven (see Romans 5:10).

2. A Right Relationship With Others

Second, the Bible sets forth the condition of right relationships with others as having an important bearing on our prayers.

Therefore if you are offering your gift at the altar and there remember that your brother has something against you, leave your gift there in front of the altar. First, go and be reconciled to your brother; then come and offer your gift.

(Matthew 5:23,24)

The Bible makes this particularly true in our families. Husbands, if you are out of harmony with your wives, the Bible says your prayers will be hindered. And that goes for wives as well. (See Ephesians 5:20-25; Colossians 3:17-19 and 2 Peter 3:1-7).

3. Repentant

Thirdly, we must recognize that if we regard iniquity in our heart, the Lord will not hear us. If there is any unconfessed sin that we are cherishing in our hearts; that we are not willing to forsake, God says He will not hear our prayers.

4. Believing

Fourthly, we must ask in faith. This means that we must trust the Lord and His working in our lives.

We must be willing to accept whatever answer God gives us without doubting His goodness or grace.

5. Asking God's Will

Fifthly, we must ask according to God's will. We cannot expect our Father to give us everything that we ask. Our attitude must be the same as Jesus' when he said, ". . . **NOT MY WILL, BUT YOURS BE DONE**" (Luke 22:42).

These five requirements of successful prayer should be carefully applied to our prayer lives.

Obstacles to Prayer

There are many reasons why people don't pray. I think the greatest of these is unbelief. We just do not believe that God will answer our prayers. The source of this unbelief is often in the prayers we have made that were not answered, because we prayed them neither according to His will nor meeting the conditions of prayer.

There is also the matter of insincerity. "The cardinal virtue of prayer," said one, "is sincerity." This means we should be absolutely and ruthlessly honest with ourselves and with God. Stay away from prayer that is selfish, petty, unspiritual and carnal. Better to first ask God for the right attitudes than to pray a selfish, sinful prayer.

To help us keep the right attitude before God, a quiet time should be set aside each day for prayer and meditation. During this time with God, we need to learn what it means to be an intercessor, to know what faith in prayer really means, and to trust God for greater things. We need to step out onto the higher plateaus of prayer.

I hope you will spend time each day with Jesus in personal prayer, and you will thereby find a new dimension in your relationship with God.

TEST YOURSELF ON CHAPTER 4

1. What does God want us to do in order to avoid anxiety?

   _____

   _____

   _____

   _____

2. What basic elements should our prayers contain?

   _____

   _____

   _____

   _____

3. What are the requirements for answered prayer?

   _____

   _____

   _____

   _____

Chapter 5

CONTINUING IN FELLOWSHIP

Fellowship is another subject of great importance to the Christian. Christian fellowship or **KOINONIA**, as it is called in the Greek text of the New Testament, is a very special aspect of the Christian life.

A key passage to remember when thinking of fellowship is 1 John 1:3,4. There we read:

> **We proclaim to you what we have seen and heard, so that you also may have fellowship with us. And our fellowship is with the Father and with his Son, Jesus Christ. We write this to make our joy complete.**

This passage teaches that God intended for us to enjoy the fellowship of other believers. This fellowship is always to be centered around our personal relationship with Christ.

As we consider the vitality and the virility of the Apostolic Church, that young body of Christians which burst forth in a decadent Roman world with such overwhelming power and strength, we note that one of the keys of its tremendously bold witness for Christ was KOINONIA or fellowship.

> **They devoted themselves to the apostles' teaching and to** *the fellowship*, **to the breaking of bread and to prayer. Everyone was filled with awe, and many wonders and miraculous signs were done by the apostles. All the believers were together and had everything in common.**

> **(Acts 2:42-44)**

Everyday they *continued to meet together* in the temple courts. They broke bread in their homes and ate together with glad and sincere hearts, praising God and enjoying the favor of all the people. And the Lord added to their number daily those who were being saved.

(Acts 2:46,47)

This type of fellowship is hard for us to understand. We live in a depersonalized world; an automated universe where men must remember their area code, zip code, social security and license plate numbers. Now, even their income tax is checked by computer. In most colleges students are known only by a number. Seldom is their name known or is there any real concern for their lives. Truly there is a great need for real fellowship today.

The Solid Union of Fellowship

Let us look at what is meant by this type of fellowship. It means a sharing of life. It means there is one life which is flowing through all of those who live in Christ Jesus.

The early Church was very much aware that in some secret, mysterious way they had been made one. They were one temple, though many living stones; one vine, though many branches; one family, though many children. They had one life which pulsed through each of their hearts. In this confluence of life they discovered something that made their lives rich and meaningful.

The basis for our fellowship — for this KOINONIA — is the living, risen, resurrected Christ. We are not fools. This is no cunningly devised fable. This is no mere sentimentality; this is a real, hard fact. Jesus is alive! He is alive, and our fellowship with Him is real now and will be forever.

If there is to be true fellowship, it must be produced by and based upon a living proclamation of the Gospel of Christ. And so fellowship springs from evangelism.

Some people today are lonely and without hope, when they could be entering into the most blessed fellowship ever known. Christian fellowship is still the greatest fellowship that has ever existed on the face of the earth!

Christ Is the Tie That Binds

The oneness that Christ Jesus puts into our hearts — the oneness with other fellow believers — is something tremendous to know and to experience. I have found that wherever I go in the world, if I run into a person who has received the living, resurrected Christ, I am his brother and he is mine.

This is a thrilling experience. Whether black or white, male or female, rich or poor — if they know the living Christ, they are a fellow Child of God, and within minutes we have a rapport that is not found among other people.

Why? Because we share the same light from Heaven. The same vitalizing principle dwells in us both. We have the same hope, for we worshiip the same Christ. This fellowship in not only with us, but also **"WITH THE FATHER, AND WITH HIS SON JESUS CHRIST"** (1 John 1:3).

The Bible says that we can have no fellowship without Christ (John 14:20,21,23; 1 John 4:5). The Scriptures declare that we cannot have God without having Christ (John 10:30,38; 1 John 2:23). The Bible says we cannot know God without knowing Christ (John 8:19; 14:6-11; 1 John 5:20). We cannot worship God unless we worship Christ (John 5:23; 8:42; 1 John 5:1). Christ is the center of true fellowship.

Our fellowship is **"WITH HIM"** (1 John 1:6). This is how we have come to know Him. This is how we have entered into this relationship of KOINONIA with God, where we share in His life and Christ shares His life in us (Galatians 2:20).

We have this mutual participation. And what a blessed fellowship it is; this fellowship, having descended vertically from God, now moves horizontally among the brethren.

Fellowship Is a Unique Source of Joy

When we have fellowship with God the Father and our Lord Jesus Christ in the communion of other believers, it creates a real joy in our hearts. Those who live a solitary Christian life and never share their lives with other Christians in spiritual fellowship, have never experienced the fullness of joy that God has for them.

Would you like to have this joy in your life? Then cultivate, seek after and pursue the fellowship of love with other Christians. We need to have a deep commitment of regularly sharing communion with other believers.

Stay in the Light

However, joyful Christian fellowship only takes place when we **"walk in the light"** (1 John 1:5,7). This is light which reveals . . . which makes transparent . . . which makes luminous, and clear. Determine by God's grace to walk in the light and not merely cover your life with a veil, hiding your secret sins from God and from one another.

The Bible teaches us to confess our faults one to another and pray for one another. But how little of this is done today. Consequently, people live behind a crusty veneer. They live lonely lives in the midst of crowds. They are unhappy without any deep friendships; having no one with whom they can share their lives. There is always pretense and hypocrisy hiding behind the mask. They never really get out into the light and let their lives flow through one another.

The Bible says we should be an encouragement to one another.

And let us consider how we may spur one another on toward love and good deeds. Let us not give up meeting together, as some are in the habit of doing, but let us encourage one another — and all the more as you see the Day approaching.

(Hebrews 10:24,25)

So, I encourage you to find a Christian fellowship and really get serious with God. Get honest with Him and with one another. What blessings you will find!

Share this new life that Christ has given you. If you have not yet found a church where Jesus Christ is lifted up and honored, where His Word is believed and proclaimed, then I encourage you to find such a church and enter fully into the services and take advantage of the opportunities of worship and study available to you there. God will richly bless you through His Word and the fellowship of other believers in Christ if you do.

TEST YOURSELF ON CHAPTER 5

1. Define KOINONIA.

   _____

   _____

   _____

   _____

2. What is the difference between Christian fellowship and any other kind of fellowship? That is, what is Christian fellowship based upon?

   _____

   _____

   _____

   _____

3. Can we have true fellowship when we are not walking closely with the Lord? Why or why not? (Use the Bible to support your answer.)

   _____

   _____

   _____

   _____

Chapter 6

CHANGING THE WORLD

In the previous chapter we considered the matter of Christian fellowship and the importance of intermingling and sharing your new life with others of like precious faith. I want now to consider the subject of the Church of Christ and its purpose and place in a modern technological society.

This is truly a new and exciting age in which we have been privileged to be born. Think of how much people in generations past would have given to live in our age and see what we see — men flying to the moon at tremendous speeds, computers able to store mountains of information, pictures of Saturn beamed into our living rooms.

This is our time — a time in which, by the providence of God we have been placed on the earth. And this is a wonderful time in which to live, in spite of all of its problems.

What about the Church of Jesus Christ in an age like this? Is it simply some archaic anachronism that doesn't belong in a modern-day world? To many, this is just the way it seems. And to many, this is just what it has become.

The Church in the World Today

Many people today pass the Church by or see it as a sleepy, dead organization, sitting on the corners of most American towns, doing very little of use in an age of tremendous feats and accomplishments. No doubt, part of the responsibility for this image rests right on the shoulders of the Church itself, because we in the Church have not been what Christ would have us to be. Yet, the Church hasn't always been the way it is today.

What, then, ought the Church of Jesus Christ to be? Look at it when it was dynamic, fresh-blown from the Master's hand. A handful of men came into a city called Thessalonica, and they hadn't been there but three Sabbath days until the whole city was in pandemonium.

The Church isn't being accused of turning the world upside down today, is it? That is really a shame! It is interesting to note that the late Peter Marshall, former chaplain of the United States Senate, used to say that when the early Christians preached, there were either riots or regenerations. I wish that were still true today.

Consider with me what the Church is like. From God's perspective, the Church of Jesus Christ is center stage in this world. Everything else is just the backdrop, the scenery for the real action — the eternal transformation of human beings.

We need to hear again the voice of Jesus Christ as He speaks to His people. We need to hear clearly the message that He brings — the message that He gave to His Church when He called His people unto Himself (Matthew 10; Mark 3:13-15, 6:7-13; Luke 9:1-6, 10:1-24). The message was, in effect, simply this: "Come, help Me change the world." And this is my challenge to you now, "Come, help Jesus change the world."

The way the world will be changed, according to Christ, is not via the method of the "social gospel"; that is, by reorganizing the affairs of men. The world is going to be permanently changed only when the hearts of men and women are changed by God.

You can take the same sinful people, shuffle them around, restack them one way or another, and reorganize them, but they are still going to be the same immoral, covetous, greedy individuals they were before, unless Christ changes their hearts.

Jesus did not preach slum clearance. He did not take men out of the slums. He took the slums out of the men, and soon men got rid of the slums. Because, you see, as a man **"THINKETH IN HIS HEART, SO IS HE"** (Proverbs 23:7). The world is what it is because of what individual human beings are in their hearts.

It is the Gospel of Jesus Christ that sets men free, that severs the bonds that holds them in captivity. The Gospel also has social impact. For example, it is the Gospel of Christ which has produced literacy in the world. To confirm this, just check the statistics. The nations where the true Gospel of Christ has been preached and accepted are the nations that have learned to read, and with that have come all the blessings of civilization. In other places where the Gospel has been chained, people languish in their ignorance.

Oh, that God would take away the blinders from our eyes so that we might see the important role Christians play in the world. Christ said that His people would be the salt and light of the world (Matthew 5:13,14). God uses Christians to help prevent the complete corruption, decay and putrefaction of this world.

The Great Commission and You

What is God's objective for the Christian Church? That objective, simply stated is:

Therefore go and make disciples of all nations, baptizing them in the name of the Father and of the Son and of the Holy Spirit, and teaching them to obey everything I have commanded you. And surely I am with you always, to the very end of the age.

(Matthew 28:19,20)

This is the Great Commission which has been given to the Church by its King. Nothing else will suffice.

Why is the Church to do this? Because God wants His name to be honored throughout the earth. He wants the whole world to be filled with the preaching of His love which was made known in the life of Jesus. He desires to call people of every nation to the light and give them the gift of eternal life. By sharing the Gospel and training disciples, God is honored and His name is glorified.

No amendments may be offered to the motion. It is not debatable. It cannot be countermanded, for it is the command of the King. It is the duty of His Church. It is the command of God for your life and mine.

You may say, "It's too big." Well, every businessman knows it is not enough just to have a definite objective and to spell it out clearly. You must also have, in addition to the long-range objective, a step-by-step procedure which will enable you to reach that goal.

The Game Plan

First, it is vital that we recognize that God will give His power to His people in order to accomplish the goal of reaching the world with the message of the Gospel of Christ (Matthew 28:18; Mark 16:15; Acts 1:8). Oh, that you would come to call, in faith, upon that great God of ours as He is the divine resource of all our needs. He can enable us to do the impossible.

But there is a human resource as well. There is a divine key which God has given for this great task to which we have been commissioned. Christ showed us the way He was going to reach the world. Jesus never traveled to Athens, never preached at the Parthenon, never went to Rome. Rather, Jesus invested His life in a small group of people. He trained them thoroughly, and He trained them to train others.

This was His key: the spiritual multiplication of the Church. Pastors realize that it is only through the training and equipping of normal everyday Christians that the job of world evangelism can be done.

God has singularly designed it so that you are one of those who can most effectively perform the Great Commission that He has given to us all. You rub shoulders every day with many unbelievers. Therefore, you should look for any opportunity you can to reach these people.

God has given pastors and teachers to the Church in order that they might equip the saints to do the work of ministering. According to the New Testament, every Christian is a saint (Ephesians 2:19), a sanctified one (1 Corinthians 1:2), a separated one (Romans 7:1), a cleansed one (Ephesians 5:26,27), and every Christian is a minister with a ministry to perform (2 Corinthians 5:17 - 6:10).

You, as a Christian have a ministry to which God has called you. And it is the ministry of the clergyman to equip you to perform more effectively the ministry which God has given to you.

Today, ministers everywhere are catching the vision, and now churches are beginning to see the important need of training and equipping church members in small groups and private Bible studies for evangelism. Also, Christians are beginning to realize that evangelism is both their privilege and their responsibility.

One of the most basic needs of the heart is the need for adventure. God made us to be great adventurers for Him. This need for adventure is what took Columbus across the ocean. This is what takes men to the moon and will take them to the stars. But the greatest adventure in all the world is to be a co-laborer with God and take men to Heaven.

Now, let us consider for a moment our short-term goal. How are we going to do this? One way is by setting an example. This begins right here at home.

By the power of God's Spirit, what can the Church be? It will come to pass that the Church will be what it ought to be when men and women are totally committed to Christ, and saying, "Lord, here is my heart, my mind, my talents, my intellect, my body, my hands, my mouth and my feet. Take them and use them for your honor and glory."

Others will hear of the Good News when the Church becomes totally committed to spreading it. What the Church needs today is millions of involved people sharing the Gospel of Christ with others.

This was the secret power of the early Church. We read that all **"THOSE WHO HAD BEEN SCATTERED PREACHED THE WORD WHEREVER THEY WENT"** (Acts 8:4). And the term used in the Greek text for "preaching" means "evangelizing," proclaiming the evangel, the tidings of the Gospel of the free grace of God.

Pass It On

In whatever capacity you find yourself, there are many opportunities to witness. If your church is like most Bible-believing churches today, they are providing opportunities for learning how to share your faith in Christ. I hope that after having received the greatest Gift in the world, you will want to pass it on. I hope you will speak to someone who knows Christ and ask how you might learn to share your faith more effectively with others so that you can become part of what truly is the greatest adventure in the world.

TEST YOURSELF ON CHAPTER 6

1. Why is the Church really the center of all human history?

   _____

   _____

   _____

   _____

2. It has been said that the "social gospel" treats only the symptoms of world problems while the pure Gospel treats the source. Explain this.

   _____

   _____

   _____

3. What did Christ mean when He called believers the "salt of the earth"? (See Matthew 5:13,14)

   _____

   _____

   _____

   _____

4. What was Jesus' key to changing the world? How does it apply today?

_____

_____

_____

_____

Chapter 7

SHARING YOUR FAITH

God has blessed my life by allowing me to share with many people the Good News about God's plan of salvation through Jesus Christ. I have made it a major part of my ministry to train other Christians to effectively communicate their personal faith in Jesus. Because of this burden, I want to also help you share your faith by explaining some key principles in communicating the Good News to others.

The beginning step in learning to share your faith with others is to learn a simple summary of the Gospel. I have developed an outline comprised of five major points which logically and clearly communicates the Christian message.

These five points are:

1. **Grace**

2. **Man**

3. **God**

4. **Christ**

5. **Faith**

Herein are represented the main ideas to be shared with anyone who needs to know the love of God. Take a moment and say them out loud: **"Grace, Man, God, Christ, Faith."** Say them again: **"Grace, Man, God, Christ, Faith."** Now close your eyes and say them. By doing this a number of times you will be able to memorize this basic outline and use it to share the message of God's love with others.

Once you have mastered the order of these five basic points, you need to add to each one of them the qualifying statements which will bring real meaning to your presentation of the Gospel.

The first point is **Grace.** We need to include two important ideas here by adding to our outline the following concepts:

1. **GRACE**

   a. Heaven is a free gift
   b. It is not earned or deserved

This is the place to start sharing the Gospel. Note that this is positive. We start with the message of God's love and His offer of eternal life in Heaven. By doing this, we focus their thoughts on what God wants to give them.

This is a fairly startling idea; at least, it will be for many of the people with whom you will be sharing. Most people think Heaven is something you earn by being good — going to church, singing in the choir, teaching Sunday school, obeying the Ten Commandments, following the Golden Rule, etc. But the fact of the matter is, Heaven is a free gift; it is not earned or deserved.

> **For it is by grace you have been saved, through faith — and this not from yourselves, it is the gift of God — not by works, so that no one can boast.**
>
> **(Ephesians 2:8,9)**

This passage teaches clearly that salvation is given to us by God. We can *never* earn it, but God has mercifully provided it for us.

Now, let us look at the second point of our outline, **Man.** This needs to be clarified with two additional concepts as well.

2. **MAN**

    a. Is a sinner
    b. Cannot save himself

That seems fairly clear. Man has broken God's law. He is a sinner and so nothing he tries to do can ever make him good enough to earn a place in Heaven.

    . . . For all have sinned and fall short of the glory of God . . .

                                      (Romans 3:23)

All of us have broken God's law. We are all in need of forgiveness.

The importance of this concept is clarified when we look at the Biblical teaching concerning **God**:

3. **GOD**

    a. God is merciful
    b. God is just

The Bible teaches that God is **merciful.** He wants us to be with Him in Heaven. He wants us, as His creatures, to have eternal life.

At the same time, God is **just.** This means that He has to judge our sins. They must be paid for if His justice is to be satisfied.

Though God **"has loved us with an everlasting love"** (Jeremiah 31:3), He **"is of purer eyes than to behold evil"** (Habakkuk 1:13) and **"will by no means clear the guilty"** (Exodus 34:7). God's love seeks to redeem the sinner while His justice demands that He fairly judge us as guilty.

The answer to this dilemma is found in the person of Jesus Christ. Again we must add some information to our outline to clarify what we mean when we talk about **Christ:**

4. **CHRIST**

   a. Who He is: The infinite-eternal God-man
   b. What He did: Died on the cross and was raised from the dead to purchase a place for us in Heaven.

God's love is clearly seen in Jesus. He became a man — though He is the eternal God. He died on a cross —though He was sinless. He died to pay for sins . . . **our sins.** In this He shows God's love and fulfills God's justice. He died and suffered the wrath of God in our stead. The Scripture teaches that Jesus was **"the Word (who) became flesh and dwelt among us"** (John 1:14) and **"was made sin for us"** (2 Corinthians 5:21) so that we might be forgiven in the sight of God.

Jesus not only died for our sins, but He was also raised from the dead. He now has the divine authority to offer eternal life to all who receive Him through **Faith:**

5. **FAITH**

   a. What it is: Trusting in Jesus Christ alone
   b. What it is not: Intellectual assent or temporal faith

Faith is the key to Heaven. **Saving faith** is trusting in Jesus Christ alone for our eternal salvation from God's punishment and accepting Him completely as Ruler of our lives. Only as we depend totally on Him can we know that God has forgiven us and made us new.

Faith is not mere intellectual assent nor superficial head-knowledge about Jesus Christ. Neither is "saving faith" only trusting God for things such as safety, health, wealth, etc., all of which are temporal and will one day pass away.

. . . Believe in the Lord Jesus and you will be saved — you and your household.

(Acts 16:31)

The promise of God is clear. All who sincerely believe (trust) in the Lord Jesus Christ will be saved.

In summary, our outline of the Gospel of God looks like this when you put it all together.

1. **GRACE**

   a. Heaven is a free gift (Romans 6:23)
   b. It is not earned or deserved (Ephesians 2:8,9)

2. **MAN**

   a. Is a sinner (Romans 3:23)
   b. Cannot save himself (Romans 3:20)

3. **GOD**

   a. Is merciful (Titus 3:5)
   b. Is just (Jeremiah 31:3, Habakkuk 1:13, Exodus 34:7)

4. **CHRIST**

   a. Who He is: The infinite-eternal God-man (John 1:1,14)
   b. What He did: Died on the cross to purchase a place for us in Heaven (Romans 3:21-26; 2 Corinthians 5:21)

5. **FAITH**

    a.   What it is: Trusting in Jesus Christ as Lord and Savior (Acts 16:31)

    b.   What it is not: Intellectual assent or temporal faith (James 2:19)

This outline provides you with the simple tool you need to clearly present the Gospel to your friends and family. Go back and read this brief outline aloud two or three times. See how logically it flows?

You can become an effective communicator of the Gospel by utlilizing such a brief outline as this. While memorizing the outline, you will come to see more clearly how each part of the Gospel is a truth which has importance to your life. Practice this outline often. Attempt to say it in your own words and begin to use examples from your life to illustrate the points it makes.

Practice each day saying it aloud as often as you think of it and meditate on the great truths of each point. Ask some Christian friends to listen to you say it. Talk through it with them and family members, embellishing the outline in your own words until you become comfortable with it.

Then, begin asking God to lead you to people who need to hear this great truth. God has promised to bring people to Himself when we share the Gospel. Armed with this knowledge, you can go with the confidence that you are equipped to talk to others who do not, as yet, understand God's grace.

Moses was a stutterer, but God used him in a mighty way to proclaim His truth. Paul did not consider himself eloquent of speech, but God blessed his faithfulness. We may perceive ourselves as the feeblest of communicators; but because the truth we have to share is God's powerful truth, He will honor our faithfulness in proclaiming the Gospel. This will be demonstrated by His giving us opportunities to share the Good News of Christ with others.

We must reach out in the love of God to share this life-changing message with everyone we have opportunity to reach. Only then will we be able to change the world from the inside out.

There are two questions that I have found which lead into a conversation about Christ and help to begin the sharing of our faith. These questions are:

1.   **Have you come to a place in your spiritual life where you know for certain that if you were to die you would go to Heaven?**

2.   **Suppose that you were to die today and stand before God and He were to say to you, "Why should I let you into my Heaven?" What would you say?**

By asking people these questions, it can help determine if the person is trusting in Jesus to save them or in their own good works. They provide a practical bridge which can help you lead the person to Christ.

Some of those with whom we share the Gospel will want to accept Jesus Christ as their Lord and Savior. We can lead them in this by helping them to pray, phrase by phrase, a simple prayer like this:

"Lord Jesus, I need you. Thank you for dying for my sins. I repent of them now and want my life to count for you. Come into my heart and make me new. Amen."

This simple prayer, sincerely said to God, can be the entry to an entirely new life.

TEST YOURSELF ON CHAPTER 7

1. From memory, list the five main parts of the Gospel outline.

   _____

   _____

   _____

2. From memory, list the entire Gospel outline — including the two concepts under each major point.

   _____

   _____

   _____

   _____

   _____

   _____

3. List, in order, the Scripture references for each of the main five points on the outline.

   _____

   _____

   _____

   _____

4. What are the two questions which may help you find an opportunity to share your faith?

(a)_____

_____

_____

(b)_____

_____

_____

PART TWO

The Gospel of John

JOHN

Author

The author is the apostle John, "the disciple whom Jesus loved" (13:23; 19:26; 20:2; 21:7,20,24). He was prominent in the early church but is not mentioned by name in this Gospel — which would be natural if he wrote it, but hard to explain otherwise. The author knew Jewish life well, as seen from references to popular Messianic speculations (e.g., 1:20-21; 7:40-42), to the hostility between Jews and Samaritans (4:9), and to Jewish customs, such as the duty of circumcision on the eighth day taking precedence over the prohibition of working on the Sabbath (see note on 7:22). He knew the geography of Palestine, locating Bethany about 15 stadia (about two miles) from Jerusalem (11:18) and mentioning Cana, a village not referred to in any earlier writing known to us (2:1; 21:2). The Gospel of John has many touches that were obviously based on the recollections of an eyewitness — such as the house at Bethany being filled with the fragrance of the broken perfume jar (12:3). Early writers such as Irenaeus and Tertullian say that John wrote this Gospel, and all other evidence agrees.

Date

In general, two views of the dating of this Gospel have been advocated:

1. The traditional view places it toward the end of the first century, c. A.D. 85 or later.

2. More recently, some scholars have suggested an earlier date, perhaps as early as the 50s and no later than 70.

The first view may be supported by reference to the statement of Clement of Alexandria that John wrote to supplement the accounts found in the other Gospels (Eusebius, *Ecclesiastical History*, 6.14.7), and thus his Gospel is later than the first three. It has also been argued that the seemingly more developed theology of the fourth Gospel indicates that it originated later.

The second view has found favor because it has been felt more recently that John wrote independently of the other Gospels. This does not contradict the statement of Clement referred to above. Also, those who hold this view point out that developed theology does not necessarily argue for a late origin. The theology of Romans (written c. 57) is every bit as developed as that in John. Further, the statement in 5:2 that there "is" (rather than "was") a pool "near the Sheep Gate" may suggest a time before 70, when Jerusalem was destroyed. Others, however, observe that John elsewhere sometimes used the present tense when speaking of the past.

Purpose and Emphases

Some interpreters have felt that John's aim was to set forth a version of the Christian message that would appeal to Greek thinkers. Others have seen a desire to supplement (or correct) the Synoptic Gospels, to combat some form of heresy, to oppose the continuing followers of John the Baptist or to achieve a similar goal. But the writer himself states his main purpose clearly: "These are written that you may believe that Jesus is the Christ, the Son of God, and that by believing you may have life in his name" (20:31). He may have had Greek readers mainly in mind, some of whom were being exposed to heretical influence, but his primary intention was evangelistic. It is possible to understand "may believe" in the sense of "may continue to believe" — in which case the purpose would be to build up believers as well as to win new converts.

For the main emphases of the book see notes on 1:4,7,10,14,19,49; 2:4,11; 3:27; 4:34; 6:35; 13:1-17:26; 13:31; 17:1-2,5; 20:31.

INTRODUCTION: John

Outline

I. Prologue (1:1-18)

II. Beginnings of Jesus' Ministry (1:19-51)

    A. The Ministry of His Forerunner (1:19-34)

    B. Jesus' Introduction to Some Future Disciples (1:35-51)

III. Jesus' Public Ministry: Signs and Discourses (chs. 2-11)

    A. Changing Water to Wine (2:1-11)

    B. Cleansing the Temple (2:12-25)

    C. Interview with Nicodemus (3:1-21)

    D. Parallel Ministry with John the Baptist (3:22-4:3)

    E. Journey through Samaria: The Woman at the Well (4:4-42)

    F. Healing of the Official's Son (4:43-54)

    G. Trip to Jerusalem for an Annual Feast (ch. 5)

    H. The Feeding of the 5,000 and the Sermon on the Bread of Life (ch.6)

    I. Jesus at the Feast of Tabernacles (chs. 7-8)

    J. Healing of the Man Born Blind (ch. 9)

    K. Parable of the Good Shepherd (10:1-21)

    L. Debating at the Feast of Dedication (10:22-39)

    M. Ministry in Perea (10:40-42)

    N. The Raising of Lazarus (ch. 11)

IV.   The Passion Week (chs. 12-19)

    A.   The Anointing of Jesus' Feet (12:1-11)
    B.   The Triumphal Entry (12:12-19)
    C.   The Coming of the Greeks (12:20-36)
    D.   Continued Jewish Unbelief (12:37-50)
    E.   Farewell Discourses (chs. 13-17)

        1.   Discourse at the Last Supper (chs. 13-14)
        2.   Discourse on the way to Gethsemane (chs. 15-16)
        3.   Jesus' prayer of intercession (ch. 17)

    F.   Jesus' Betrayal and Arrest (18:1-12)
    G.   The Trials of Jesus (18:13-19:15)
    H.   The Crucifixion and Burial (19:16-42)

V.   The Resurrection (20:1-29)

VI.   The Statement of Purpose (20:30-31)

VII.   Epilogue (ch. 21)

John

The Word Became Flesh

1 In the beginning was the Word, and the Word was with God, and the Word was God. ²He was with God in the beginning. ³Through him all things were made; without him nothing was made that has been made. ⁴In him was life, and that life was the light of men. ⁵The light shines in the darkness, but the darkness has not understood *a* it.

⁶There came a man who was sent from God; his name was John. ⁷He came as a witness to testify concerning that light, so that through him all men might believe. ⁸He himself was not the light; he came only as a witness to the light. ⁹The true light that gives light to every man was coming into the world. *b*

¹⁰He was in the world, and though the world was made through him, the world did not recognize him. ¹¹He came to that which was his own, but his own did not receive him. ¹²Yet to all who received him, to those who believed in his name, he gave the right to become children of God— ¹³children born not of natural descent, *c* nor of human decision or a husband's will, but born of God.

¹⁴The Word became flesh and made his dwelling among us. We have seen his glory, the glory of the One and Only, *d* who came from the Father, full of grace and truth.

¹⁵John testifies concerning him. He cries out, saying, "This was he of whom I said, 'He who comes after me has surpassed me because he was before me.' " ¹⁶From the fullness of his grace we have all received one blessing after another. ¹⁷For the law was given through Moses; grace and truth came through Jesus Christ. ¹⁸No one has ever seen God, but God the One and Only, *d,e* who is at the Father's side, has made him known.

John the Baptist Denies Being the Christ

¹⁹Now this was John's testimony when the Jews of Jerusalem

a5 Or darkness, and the darkness has not overcome   *b9 Or This was the true light that gives light to every man who comes into the world*   *c13 Greek of bloods*   *d14,18 Or the Only Begotten*   *e18 Some manuscripts but the only (or only begotten) Son*

ent priests and Levites to ask him who he was. ²⁰He did not fail
to confess, but confessed freely, "I am not the Christ. *a*"

²¹They asked him, "Then who are you? Are you Elijah?"
He said, "I am not."

"Are you the Prophet?"
He answered, "No."

²²Finally they said, "Who are you? Give us an answer to take
back to those who sent us. What do you say about yourself?"

²³John replied in the words of Isaiah the prophet, "I am the
voice of one calling in the desert, 'Make straight the way for the
Lord.' " *b*

²⁴Now some Pharisees who had been sent ²⁵questioned him,
"Why then do you baptize if you are not the Christ, nor Elijah,
nor the Prophet?"

²⁶"I baptize with *c* water," John replied, "but among you stands
one you do not know. ²⁷He is the one who comes after me, the
thongs of whose sandals I am not worthy to untie."

²⁸This all happened at Bethany on the other side of the Jor-
dan, where John was baptizing.

Jesus the Lamb of God

²⁹The next day John saw Jesus coming toward him and said,
"Look, the Lamb of God, who takes away the sin of the world!
³⁰This is the one I meant when I said, 'A man who comes after
me has surpassed me because he was before me.' ³¹I myself
did not know him, but the reason I came baptizing with water
was that he might be revealed to Israel."

³²Then John gave this testimony: "I saw the Spirit come down
from heaven as a dove and remain on him. ³³I would not have
known him, except that the one who sent me to baptize with
water told me, 'The man on whom you see the Spirit come down
and remain is he who will baptize with the Holy Spirit.' ³⁴I have
seen and I testify that this is the Son of God."

Jesus' First Disciples

³⁵The next day John was there again with two of his disciples.
³⁶When he saw Jesus passing by, he said, "Look, the Lamb of
God!"

---

a20 Or *Messiah.* "The Christ" (Greek) and "the Messiah" (Hebrew) both mean
"the Anointed One"; also in verse 25.   *b23* Isaiah 40:3   *c26* Or *in*;
also in verses 31 and 33

³⁷When the two disciples heard him say this, they followed Jesus. ³⁸Turning around, Jesus saw them following and asked, "What do you want?"

They said, "Rabbi" (which means Teacher), "where are you staying?"

³⁹"Come," he replied, "and you will see."

So they went and saw where he was staying, and spent that day with him. It was about the tenth hour.

⁴⁰Andrew, Simon Peter's brother, was one of the two who heard what John had said and who had followed Jesus. ⁴¹The first thing Andrew did was to find his brother Simon and tell him, "We have found the Messiah" (that is, the Christ). ⁴²And he brought him to Jesus.

Jesus looked at him and said, "You are Simon son of John. You will be called Cephas" (which, when translated, is Peter ᵃ).

Jesus Calls Philip and Nathanael

⁴³The next day Jesus decided to leave for Galilee. Finding Philip, he said to him, "Follow me."

⁴⁴Philip, like Andrew and Peter, was from the town of Bethsaida. ⁴⁵Philip found Nathanael and told him, "We have found the one Moses wrote about in the Law, and about whom the prophets also wrote—Jesus of Nazareth, the son of Joseph."

⁴⁶"Nazareth! Can anything good come from there?" Nathanael asked.

"Come and see," said Philip.

⁴⁷When Jesus saw Nathanael approaching, he said of him, "Here is a true Israelite, in whom there is nothing false."

⁴⁸"How do you know me?" Nathanael asked.

Jesus answered, "I saw you while you were still under the fig tree before Philip called you."

⁴⁹Then Nathanael declared, "Rabbi, you are the Son of God; you are the King of Israel."

⁵⁰Jesus said, "You believe ᵇ because I told you I saw you under the fig tree. You shall see greater things than that." ⁵¹He then added, "I tell you ᶜ the truth, you ᶜ shall see heaven open, and the angels of God ascending and descending on the Son of Man."

ᵃ42 Both *Cephas* (Aramaic) and *Peter* (Greek) mean *rock*.   ᵇ50 Or *Do you believe . . . ?*   ᶜ51 The Greek is plural.

Jesus Changes Water to Wine

2 On the third day a wedding took place at Cana in Galilee. Jesus' mother was there, [2]and Jesus and his disciples had also been invited to the wedding. [3]When the wine was gone, Jesus' mother said to him, "They have no more wine."

[4]"Dear woman, why do you involve me?" Jesus replied. "My time has not yet come."

[5]His mother said to the servants, "Do whatever he tells you."

[6]Nearby stood six stone water jars, the kind used by the Jews for ceremonial washing, each holding from twenty to thirty gallons. [a]

[7]Jesus said to the servants, "Fill the jars with water"; so they filled them to the brim.

[8]Then he told them, "Now draw some out and take it to the master of the banquet."

They did so, [9]and the master of the banquet tasted the water that had been turned into wine. He did not realize where it had come from, though the servants who had drawn the water knew. Then he called the bridegroom aside [10]and said, "Everyone brings out the choice wine first and then the cheaper wine after the guests have had too much to drink; but you have saved the best till now."

[11]This, the first of his miraculous signs, Jesus performed in Cana of Galilee. He thus revealed his glory, and his disciples put their faith in him.

Jesus Clears the Temple

[12]After this he went down to Capernaum with his mother and brothers and his disciples. There they stayed for a few days.

[13]When it was almost time for the Jewish Passover, Jesus went up to Jerusalem. [14]In the temple courts he found men selling cattle, sheep and doves, and others sitting at tables exchanging money. [15]So he made a whip out of cords, and drove all from the temple area, both sheep and cattle; he scattered the coins of the money changers and overturned their tables. [16]To those who sold doves he said, "Get these out of here! How dare you turn my Father's house into a market!"

[17]His disciples remembered that it is written: "Zeal for your house will consume me." [b]

---

[a]6 Greek *two to three metretes* (probably about 75 to 115 liters)
[b]17 Psalm 69:9

¹⁸Then the Jews demanded of him, "What miraculous sign can you show us to prove your authority to do all this?"

¹⁹Jesus answered them, "Destroy this temple, and I will raise it again in three days."

²⁰The Jews replied, "It has taken forty-six years to build this temple, and you are going to raise it in three days?" ²¹But the temple he had spoken of was his body. ²²After he was raised from the dead, his disciples recalled what he had said. Then they believed the Scripture and the words that Jesus had spoken.

²³Now while he was in Jerusalem at the Passover Feast, many people saw the miraculous signs he was doing and believed in his name. ᵃ ²⁴But Jesus would not entrust himself to them, for he knew all men. ²⁵He did not need man's testimony about man, for he knew what was in a man.

Jesus Teaches Nicodemus

3 Now there was a man of the Pharisees named Nicodemus, a member of the Jewish ruling council. ²He came to Jesus at night and said, "Rabbi, we know you are a teacher who has come from God. For no one could perform the miraculous signs you are doing if God were not with him."

³In reply Jesus declared, "I tell you the truth, no one can see the kingdom of God unless he is born again. ᵇ"

⁴"How can a man be born when he is old?" Nicodemus asked. "Surely he cannot enter a second time into his mother's womb to be born!"

⁵Jesus answered, "I tell you the truth, no one can enter the kingdom of God unless he is born of water and the Spirit. ⁶Flesh gives birth to flesh, but the Spirit ᶜ gives birth to spirit. ⁷You should not be surprised at my saying, 'You ᵈ must be born again.' ⁸The wind blows wherever it pleases. You hear its sound, but you cannot tell where it comes from or where it is going. So it is with everyone born of the Spirit."

⁹"How can this be?" Nicodemus asked.

¹⁰"You are Israel's teacher," said Jesus, "and do you not understand these things? ¹¹I tell you the truth, we speak of what we know, and we testify to what we have seen, but still you people do not accept our testimony. ¹²I have spoken to you of earthly things and you do not believe; how then will you believe

---

ᵃ23 Or and believed in him   ᵇ3 Or born from above; also in verse 7
ᶜ6 Or but spirit   ᵈ7 The Greek is plural.

if I speak of heavenly things? [13]No one has ever gone into heaven except the one who came from heaven—the Son of Man. [a] [14]Just as Moses lifted up the snake in the desert, so the Son of Man must be lifted up, [15]that everyone who believes in him may have eternal life. [b]

[16]"For God so loved the world that he gave his one and only Son, [c] that whoever believes in him shall not perish but have eternal life. [17]For God did not send his Son into the world to condemn the world, but to save the world through him. [18]Whoever believes in him is not condemned, but whoever does not believe stands condemned already because he has not believed in the name of God's one and only Son. [d] [19]This is the verdict: Light has come into the world, but men loved darkness instead of light because their deeds were evil. [20]Everyone who does evil hates the light, and will not come into the light for fear that his deeds will be exposed. [21]But whoever lives by the truth comes into the light, so that it may be seen plainly that what he has done has been done through God." [e]

John the Baptist's Testimony About Jesus

[22]After this, Jesus and his disciples went out into the Judean countryside, where he spent some time with them, and baptized. [23]Now John also was baptizing at Aenon near Salim, because there was plenty of water, and people were constantly coming to be baptized. [24](This was before John was put in prison.) [25]An argument developed between some of John's disciples and a certain Jew [f] over the matter of ceremonial washing. [26]They came to John and said to him, "Rabbi, that man who was with you on the other side of the Jordan—the one you testified about—well, he is baptizing, and everyone is going to him."

[27]To this John replied, "A man can receive only what is given him from heaven. [28]You yourselves can testify that I said, 'I am not the Christ [g] but am sent ahead of him.' [29]The bride belongs to the bridegroom. The friend who attends the bridegroom waits and listens for him, and is full of joy when he hears the bridegroom's voice. That joy is mine, and it is now complete. [30]He must become greater; I must become less.

[31]"The one who comes from above is above all; the one who is from the earth belongs to the earth, and speaks as one from

---

[a]13 Some manuscripts *Man, who is in heaven*   [b]15 Or *believes may have eternal life in him*   [c]16 Or *his only begotten Son*   [d]18 Or *God's only begotten Son*   [e]21 Some interpreters end the quotation after verse 15.
[f]25 Some manuscripts *and certain Jews*   [g]28 Or *Messiah*

the earth. The one who comes from heaven is above all. ³²He testifies to what he has seen and heard, but no one accepts his testimony. ³³The man who has accepted it has certified that God is truthful. ³⁴For the one whom God has sent speaks the words of God, for God *a* gives the Spirit without limit. ³⁵The Father loves the Son and has placed everything in his hands. ³⁶Whoever believes in the Son has eternal life, but whoever rejects the Son will not see life, for God's wrath remains on him." *b*

Jesus Talks With a Samaritan Woman

4 The Pharisees heard that Jesus was gaining and baptizing more disciples than John, ²although in fact it was not Jesus who baptized, but his disciples. ³When the Lord learned of this, he left Judea and went back once more to Galilee.

⁴Now he had to go through Samaria. ⁵So he came to a town in Samaria called Sychar, near the plot of ground Jacob had given to his son Joseph. ⁶Jacob's well was there, and Jesus, tired as he was from the journey, sat down by the well. It was about the sixth hour.

⁷When a Samaritan woman came to draw water, Jesus said to her, "Will you give me a drink?" ⁸(His disciples had gone into the town to buy food.)

⁹The Samaritan woman said to him, "You are a Jew and I am a Samaritan woman. How can you ask me for a drink?" (For Jews do not associate with Samaritans. *c*)

¹⁰Jesus answered her, "If you knew the gift of God and who it is that asks you for a drink, you would have asked him and he would have given you living water."

¹¹"Sir," the woman said, "you have nothing to draw with and the well is deep. Where can you get this living water? ¹²Are you greater than our father Jacob, who gave us the well and drank from it himself, as did also his sons and his flocks and herds?"

¹³Jesus answered, "Everyone who drinks this water will be thirsty again, ¹⁴but whoever drinks the water I give him will never thirst. Indeed, the water I give him will become in him a spring of water welling up to eternal life."

¹⁵The woman said to him, "Sir, give me this water so that I won't get thirsty and have to keep coming here to draw water."

¹⁶He told her, "Go, call your husband and come back."

¹⁷"I have no husband," she replied.

---

a34 Greek *he*   *b36* Some interpreters end the quotation after verse 30.
c9 Or *do not use dishes Samaritans have used*

Jesus said to her, "You are right when you say you have no husband. ¹⁸The fact is, you have had five husbands, and the man you now have is not your husband. What you have just said is quite true."

¹⁹"Sir," the woman said, "I can see that you are a prophet. ²⁰Our fathers worshiped on this mountain, but you Jews claim that the place where we must worship is in Jerusalem."

²¹Jesus declared, "Believe me, woman, a time is coming when you will worship the Father neither on this mountain nor in Jerusalem. ²²You Samaritans worship what you do not know; we worship what we do know, for salvation is from the Jews. ²³Yet a time is coming and has now come when the true worshipers will worship the Father in spirit and truth, for they are the kind of worshipers the Father seeks. ²⁴God is spirit, and his worshipers must worship in spirit and in truth."

²⁵The woman said, "I know that Messiah" (called Christ) "is coming. When he comes, he will explain everything to us."

²⁶Then Jesus declared, "I who speak to you am he."

The Disciples Rejoin Jesus

²⁷Just then his disciples returned and were surprised to find him talking with a woman. But no one asked, "What do you want?" or "Why are you talking with her?"

²⁸Then, leaving her water jar, the woman went back to the town and said to the people, ²⁹"Come, see a man who told me everything I ever did. Could this be the Christ ᵃ?" ³⁰They came out of the town and made their way toward him.

³¹Meanwhile his disciples urged him, "Rabbi, eat something."

³²But he said to them, "I have food to eat that you know nothing about."

³³Then his disciples said to each other, "Could someone have brought him food?"

³⁴"My food," said Jesus, "is to do the will of him who sent me and to finish his work. ³⁵Do you not say, 'Four months more and then the harvest'? I tell you, open your eyes and look at the fields! They are ripe for harvest. ³⁶Even now the reaper draws his wages, even now he harvests the crop for eternal life, so that the sower and the reaper may be glad together. ³⁷Thus the saying 'One sows and another reaps' is true. ³⁸I sent you to reap what you have not worked for. Others have done the hard work, and you have reaped the benefits of their labor."

ᵃ29 Or Messiah

Many Samaritans Believe

39Many of the Samaritans from that town believed in him because of the woman's testimony, "He told me everything I ever did." 40So when the Samaritans came to him, they urged him to stay with them, and he stayed two days. 41And because of his words many more became believers.

42They said to the woman, "We no longer believe just because of what you said; now we have heard for ourselves, and we know that this man really is the Savior of the world."

Jesus Heals the Official's Son

43After the two days he left for Galilee. 44(Now Jesus himself had pointed out that a prophet has no honor in his own country.) 45When he arrived in Galilee, the Galileans welcomed him. They had seen all that he had done in Jerusalem at the Passover Feast, for they also had been there.

46Once more he visited Cana in Galilee, where he had turned the water into wine. And there was a certain royal official whose son lay sick at Capernaum. 47When this man heard that Jesus had arrived in Galilee from Judea, he went to him and begged him to come and heal his son, who was close to death.

48"Unless you people see miraculous signs and wonders," Jesus told him, "you will never believe."

49The royal official said, "Sir, come down before my child dies."

50Jesus replied, "You may go. Your son will live."

The man took Jesus at his word and departed. 51While he was still on the way, his servants met him with the news that his boy was living. 52When he inquired as to the time when his son got better, they said to him, "The fever left him yesterday at the seventh hour."

53Then the father realized that this was the exact time at which Jesus had said to him, "Your son will live." So he and all his household believed.

54This was the second miraculous sign that Jesus performed, having come from Judea to Galilee.

The Healing at the Pool

5 Some time later, Jesus went up to Jerusalem for a feast of the Jews. 2Now there is in Jerusalem near the Sheep Gate a pool, which in Aramaic is called Bethesda a and which is

a2 Some manuscripts Bethzatha; other manuscripts Bethsaida

surrounded by five covered colonnades. ³Here a great number of disabled people used to lie—the blind, the lame, the paralyzed. *ᵃ* ⁵One who was there had been an invalid for thirty-eight years. ⁶When Jesus saw him lying there and learned that he had been in this condition for a long time, he asked him, "Do you want to get well?"

⁷"Sir," the invalid replied, "I have no one to help me into the pool when the water is stirred. While I am trying to get in, someone else goes down ahead of me."

⁸Then Jesus said to him, "Get up! Pick up your mat and walk." ⁹At once the man was cured; he picked up his mat and walked.

The day on which this took place was a Sabbath, ¹⁰and so the Jews said to the man who had been healed, "It is the Sabbath; the law forbids you to carry your mat."

¹¹But he replied, "The man who made me well said to me, 'Pick up your mat and walk.'"

¹²So they asked him, "Who is this fellow who told you to pick it up and walk?"

¹³The man who was healed had no idea who it was, for Jesus had slipped away into the crowd that was there.

¹⁴Later Jesus found him at the temple and said to him, "See, you are well again. Stop sinning or something worse may happen to you." ¹⁵The man went away and told the Jews that it was Jesus who had made him well.

Life Through the Son

¹⁶So, because Jesus was doing these things on the Sabbath, the Jews persecuted him. ¹⁷Jesus said to them, "My Father is always at his work to this very day, and I, too, am working." ¹⁸For this reason the Jews tried all the harder to kill him; not only was he breaking the Sabbath, but he was even calling God his own Father, making himself equal with God.

¹⁹Jesus gave them this answer: "I tell you the truth, the Son can do nothing by himself; he can do only what he sees his Father doing, because whatever the Father does the Son also does. ²⁰For the Father loves the Son and shows him all he does. Yes, to your amazement he will show him even greater things than these. ²¹For just as the Father raises the dead and gives them life, even so the Son gives life to whom he is pleased to

---

ᵃ3 Some less important manuscripts paralyzed—and they waited for the moving of the waters. ⁴From time to time an angel of the Lord would come down and stir up the waters. The first one into the pool after each such disturbance would be cured of whatever disease he had.

give it. ²²Moreover, the Father judges no one, but has entrusted all judgment to the Son, ²³that all may honor the Son just as they honor the Father. He who does not honor the Son does not honor the Father, who sent him.

²⁴"I tell you the truth, whoever hears my word and believes him who sent me has eternal life and will not be condemned; he has crossed over from death to life. ²⁵I tell you the truth, a time is coming and has now come when the dead will hear the voice of the Son of God and those who hear will live. ²⁶For as the Father has life in himself, so he has granted the Son to have life in himself. ²⁷And he has given him authority to judge because he is the Son of Man.

²⁸"Do not be amazed at this, for a time is coming when all who are in their graves will hear his voice ²⁹and come out—those who have done good will rise to live, and those who have done evil will rise to be condemned. ³⁰By myself I can do nothing; I judge only as I hear, and my judgment is just, for I seek not to please myself but him who sent me.

Testimonies About Jesus

³¹"If I testify about myself, my testimony is not valid. ³²There is another who testifies in my favor, and I know that his testimony about me is valid.

³³"You have sent to John and he has testified to the truth. ³⁴Not that I accept human testimony; but I mention it that you may be saved. ³⁵John was a lamp that burned and gave light, and you chose for a time to enjoy his light.

³⁶"I have testimony weightier than that of John. For the very work that the Father has given me to finish, and which I am doing, testifies that the Father has sent me. ³⁷And the Father who sent me has himself testified concerning me. You have never heard his voice nor seen his form, ³⁸nor does his word dwell in you, for you do not believe the one he sent. ³⁹You diligently study ᵃ the Scriptures because you think that by them you possess eternal life. These are the Scriptures that testify about me, ⁴⁰yet you refuse to come to me to have life.

⁴¹"I do not accept praise from men, ⁴²but I know you. I know that you do not have the love of God in your hearts. ⁴³I have come in my Father's name, and you do not accept me; but if someone else comes in his own name, you will accept him. ⁴⁴How can you believe if you accept praise from one another,

ᵃ39 Or *Study diligently* (the imperative)

yet make no effort to obtain the praise that comes from the only God *a*?

45"But do not think I will accuse you before the Father. Your accuser is Moses, on whom your hopes are set. 46If you believed Moses, you would believe me, for he wrote about me. 47But since you do not believe what he wrote, how are you going to believe what I say?"

Jesus Feeds the Five Thousand

6 Some time after this, Jesus crossed to the far shore of the Sea of Galilee (that is, the Sea of Tiberias), 2and a great crowd of people followed him because they saw the miraculous signs he had performed on the sick. 3Then Jesus went up on a mountainside and sat down with his disciples. 4The Jewish Passover Feast was near.

5When Jesus looked up and saw a great crowd coming toward him, he said to Philip, "Where shall we buy bread for these people to eat?" 6He asked this only to test him, for he already had in mind what he was going to do.

7Philip answered him, "Eight months' wages *b* would not buy enough bread for each one to have a bite!"

8Another of his disciples, Andrew, Simon Peter's brother, spoke up, 9"Here is a boy with five small barley loaves and two small fish, but how far will they go among so many?"

10Jesus said, "Have the people sit down." There was plenty of grass in that place, and the men sat down, about five thousand of them. 11Jesus then took the loaves, gave thanks, and distributed to those who were seated as much as they wanted. He did the same with the fish.

12When they had all had enough to eat, he said to his disciples, "Gather the pieces that are left over. Let nothing be wasted." 13So they gathered them and filled twelve baskets with the pieces of the five barley loaves left over by those who had eaten.

14After the people saw the miraculous sign that Jesus did, they began to say, "Surely this is the Prophet who is to come into the world." 15Jesus, knowing that they intended to come and make him king by force, withdrew again to a mountain by himself.

Jesus Walks on the Water

16When evening came, his disciples went down to the lake,

---

*a*44 Some early manuscripts *the Only One*   *b*7 Greek *two hundred denarii*

17where they got into a boat and set off across the lake for Capernaum. By now it was dark, and Jesus had not yet joined them. 18A strong wind was blowing and the waters grew rough. 19When they had rowed three or three and a half miles, *a* they saw Jesus approaching the boat, walking on the water; and they were terrified. 20But he said to them, "It is I; don't be afraid." 21Then they were willing to take him into the boat, and immediately the boat reached the shore where they were heading.

22The next day the crowd that had stayed on the opposite shore of the lake realized that only one boat had been there, and that Jesus had not entered it with his disciples, but that they had gone away alone. 23Then some boats from Tiberias landed near the place where the people had eaten the bread after the Lord had given thanks. 24Once the crowd realized that neither Jesus nor his disciples were there, they got into the boats and went to Capernaum in search of Jesus.

Jesus the Bread of Life

25When they found him on the other side of the lake, they asked him, "Rabbi, when did you get here?"

26Jesus answered, "I tell you the truth, you are looking for me, not because you saw miraculous signs but because you ate the loaves and had your fill. 27Do not work for food that spoils, but for food that endures to eternal life, which the Son of Man will give you. On him God the Father has placed his seal of approval."

28Then they asked him, "What must we do to do the works God requires?"

29Jesus answered, "The work of God is this: to believe in the one he has sent."

30So they asked him, "What miraculous sign then will you give that we may see it and believe you? What will you do? 31Our forefathers ate the manna in the desert; as it is written: 'He gave them bread from heaven to eat.' *b*"

32Jesus said to them, "I tell you the truth, it is not Moses who has given you the bread from heaven, but it is my Father who gives you the true bread from heaven. 33For the bread of God is he who comes down from heaven and gives life to the world."

34"Sir," they said, "from now on give us this bread."

35Then Jesus declared, "I am the bread of life. He who comes

---

a19 Greek *rowed twenty-five or thirty stadia* (about 5 or 6 kilometers)
b31 Exodus 16:4; Neh. 9:15; Psalm 78:24,25

to me will never go hungry, and he who believes in me will never be thirsty. 36But as I told you, you have seen me and still you do not believe. 37All that the Father gives me will come to me, and whoever comes to me I will never drive away. 38For I have come down from heaven not to do my will but to do the will of him who sent me. 39And this is the will of him who sent me, that I shall lose none of all that he has given me, but raise them up at the last day. 40For my Father's will is that everyone who looks to the Son and believes in him shall have eternal life, and I will raise him up at the last day."

41At this the Jews began to grumble about him because he said, "I am the bread that came down from heaven." 42They said, "Is this not Jesus, the son of Joseph, whose father and mother we know? How can he now say, 'I came down from heaven'?"

43"Stop grumbling among yourselves," Jesus answered. 44"No one can come to me unless the Father who sent me draws him, and I will raise him up at the last day. 45It is written in the Prophets: 'They will all be taught by God.' *a* Everyone who listens to the Father and learns from him comes to me. 46No one has seen the Father except the one who is from God; only he has seen the Father. 47I tell you the truth, he who believes has everlasting life. 48I am the bread of life. 49Your forefathers ate the manna in the desert, yet they died. 50But here is the bread that comes down from heaven, which a man may eat and not die. 51I am the living bread that came down from heaven. If anyone eats of this bread, he will live forever. This bread is my flesh, which I will give for the life of the world."

52Then the Jews began to argue sharply among themselves, "How can this man give us his flesh to eat?"

53Jesus said to them, "I tell you the truth, unless you eat the flesh of the Son of Man and drink his blood, you have no life in you. 54Whoever eats my flesh and drinks my blood has eternal life, and I will raise him up at the last day. 55For my flesh is real food and my blood is real drink. 56Whoever eats my flesh and drinks my blood remains in me, and I in him. 57Just as the living Father sent me and I live because of the Father, so the one who feeds on me will live because of me. 58This is the bread that came down from heaven. Your forefathers ate manna and died, but he who feeds on this bread will live forever." 59He said this while teaching in the synagogue in Capernaum.

a*45* Isaiah 54:13

Many Disciples Desert Jesus

60On hearing it, many of his disciples said, "This is a hard teaching. Who can accept it?"

61Aware that his disciples were grumbling about this, Jesus said to them, "Does this offend you? 62What if you see the Son of Man ascend to where he was before! 63The Spirit gives life; the flesh counts for nothing. The words I have spoken to you are spirit *a* and they are life. 64Yet there are some of you who do not believe." For Jesus had known from the beginning which of them did not believe and who would betray him. 65He went on to say, "This is why I told you that no one can come to me unless the Father has enabled him."

66From this time many of his disciples turned back and no longer followed him.

67"You do not want to leave too, do you?" Jesus asked the Twelve.

68Simon Peter answered him, "Lord, to whom shall we go? You have the words of eternal life. 69We believe and know that you are the Holy One of God."

70Then Jesus replied, "Have I not chosen you, the Twelve? Yet one of you is a devil!" 71(He meant Judas, the son of Simon Iscariot, who, though one of the Twelve, was later to betray him.)

Jesus Goes to the Feast of Tabernacles

7 After this, Jesus went around in Galilee, purposely staying away from Judea because the Jews there were waiting to take his life. 2But when the Jewish Feast of Tabernacles was near, 3Jesus' brothers said to him, "You ought to leave here and go to Judea, so that your disciples may see the miracles you do. 4No one who wants to become a public figure acts in secret. Since you are doing these things, show yourself to the world." 5For even his own brothers did not believe in him.

6Therefore Jesus told them, "The right time for me has not yet come; for you any time is right. 7The world cannot hate you, but it hates me because I testify that what it does is evil. 8You go to the Feast. I am not yet *b* going up to this Feast, because for me the right time has not yet come." 9Having said this, he stayed in Galilee.

10However, after his brothers had left for the Feast, he went also, not publicly, but in secret. 11Now at the Feast the Jews were watching for him and asking, "Where is that man?"

a63 Or *Spirit*   *b8* Some early manuscripts do not have *yet.*

¹²Among the crowds there was widespread whispering about him. Some said, "He is a good man."

Others replied, "No, he deceives the people." ¹³But no one would say anything publicly about him for fear of the Jews.

Jesus Teaches at the Feast

¹⁴Not until halfway through the Feast did Jesus go up to the temple courts and begin to teach. ¹⁵The Jews were amazed and asked, "How did this man get such learning without having studied?"

¹⁶Jesus answered, "My teaching is not my own. It comes from him who sent me. ¹⁷If anyone chooses to do God's will, he will find out whether my teaching comes from God or whether I speak on my own. ¹⁸He who speaks on his own does so to gain honor for himself, but he who works for the honor of the one who sent him is a man of truth; there is nothing false about him. ¹⁹Has not Moses given you the law? Yet not one of you keeps the law. Why are you trying to kill me?"

²⁰"You are demon-possessed," the crowd answered. "Who is trying to kill you?"

²¹Jesus said to them, "I did one miracle, and you are all astonished. ²²Yet, because Moses gave you circumcision (though actually it did not come from Moses, but from the patriarchs), you circumcise a child on the Sabbath. ²³Now if a child can be circumcised on the Sabbath so that the law of Moses may not be broken, why are you angry with me for healing the whole man on the Sabbath? ²⁴Stop judging by mere appearances, and make a right judgment."

Is Jesus the Christ?

²⁵At that point some of the people of Jerusalem began to ask, "Isn't this the man they are trying to kill? ²⁶Here he is, speaking publicly, and they are not saying a word to him. Have the authorities really concluded that he is the Christ *a*? ²⁷But we know where this man is from; when the Christ comes, no one will know where he is from."

²⁸Then Jesus, still teaching in the temple courts, cried out, "Yes, you know me, and you know where I am from. I am not here on my own, but he who sent me is true. You do not know him, ²⁹but I know him because I am from him and he sent me."

³⁰At this they tried to seize him, but no one laid a hand on him,

---

a26 Or *Messiah*; also in verses 27, 31, 41 and 42

because his time had not yet come. 31Still, many in the crowd put their faith in him. They said, "When the Christ comes, will he do more miraculous signs than this man?"

32The Pharisees heard the crowd whispering such things about him. Then the chief priests and the Pharisees sent temple guards to arrest him.

33Jesus said, "I am with you for only a short time, and then I go to the one who sent me. 34You will look for me, but you will not find me; and where I am, you cannot come."

35The Jews said to one another, "Where does this man intend to go that we cannot find him? Will he go where our people live scattered among the Greeks, and teach the Greeks? 36What did he mean when he said, 'You will look for me, but you will not find me,' and 'Where I am, you cannot come'?"

37On the last and greatest day of the Feast, Jesus stood and said in a loud voice, "If anyone is thirsty, let him come to me and drink. 38Whoever believes in me, as *a* the Scripture has said, streams of living water will flow from within him." 39By this he meant the Spirit, whom those who believed in him were later to receive. Up to that time the Spirit had not been given, since Jesus had not yet been glorified.

40On hearing his words, some of the people said, "Surely this man is the Prophet."

41Others said, "He is the Christ."

Still others asked, "How can the Christ come from Galilee? 42Does not the Scripture say that the Christ will come from David's family *b* and from Bethlehem, the town where David lived?" 43Thus the people were divided because of Jesus. 44Some wanted to seize him, but no one laid a hand on him.

Unbelief of the Jewish Leaders

45Finally the temple guards went back to the chief priests and Pharisees, who asked them, "Why didn't you bring him in?"

46"No one ever spoke the way this man does," the guards declared.

47"You mean he has deceived you also?" the Pharisees retorted. 48"Has any of the rulers or of the Pharisees believed in him? 49No! But this mob that knows nothing of the law—there is a curse on them."

50Nicodemus, who had gone to Jesus earlier and who was

---

*a*37,38 Or / If anyone is thirsty, let him come to me. / And let him drink, 38who believes in me. / As   *b*42 Greek seed

one of their own number, asked, ⁵¹"Does our law condemn anyone without first hearing him to find out what he is doing?"

⁵²They replied, "Are you from Galilee, too? Look into it, and you will find that a prophet ᵃ does not come out of Galilee."

[The earliest and most reliable manuscripts and other ancient witnesses do not have John 7:53-8:11.]

⁵³Then each went to his own home.

8 But Jesus went to the Mount of Olives. ²At dawn he appeared again in the temple courts, where all the people gathered around him, and he sat down to teach them. ³The teachers of the law and the Pharisees brought in a woman caught in adultery. They made her stand before the group ⁴and said to Jesus, "Teacher, this woman was caught in the act of adultery. ⁵In the Law Moses commanded us to stone such women. Now what do you say?" ⁶They were using this question as a trap, in order to have a basis for accusing him.

But Jesus bent down and started to write on the ground with his finger. ⁷When they kept on questioning him, he straightened up and said to them, "If any one of you is without sin, let him be the first to throw a stone at her." ⁸Again he stooped down and wrote on the ground.

⁹At this, those who heard began to go away one at a time, the older ones first, until only Jesus was left, with the woman still standing there. ¹⁰Jesus straightened up and asked her, "Woman, where are they? Has no one condemned you?"

¹¹"No one, sir," she said.

"Then neither do I condemn you," Jesus declared. "Go now and leave your life of sin."

The Validity of Jesus' Testimony

¹²When Jesus spoke again to the people, he said, "I am the light of the world. Whoever follows me will never walk in darkness, but will have the light of life."

¹³The Pharisees challenged him, "Here you are, appearing as your own witness; your testimony is not valid."

ᵃ52 Two early manuscripts *the Prophet*

¹⁴Jesus answered, "Even if I testify on my own behalf, my testimony is valid, for I know where I came from and where I am going. But you have no idea where I come from or where I am going. ¹⁵You judge by human standards; I pass judgment on no one. ¹⁶But if I do judge, my decisions are right, because I am not alone. I stand with the Father, who sent me. ¹⁷In your own Law it is written that the testimony of two men is valid. ¹⁸I am one who testifies for myself; my other witness is the Father, who sent me."

¹⁹Then they asked him, "Where is your father?"

"You do not know me or my Father," Jesus replied. "If you knew me, you would know my Father also." ²⁰He spoke these words while teaching in the temple area near the place where the offerings were put. Yet no one seized him, because his time had not yet come.

²¹Once more Jesus said to them, "I am going away, and you will look for me, and you will die in your sin. Where I go, you cannot come."

²²This made the Jews ask, "Will he kill himself? Is that why he says, 'Where I go, you cannot come'?"

²³But he continued, "You are from below; I am from above. You are of this world; I am not of this world. ²⁴I told you that you would die in your sins; if you do not believe that I am ˌthe one I claim to beˌ, ᵃ you will indeed die in your sins."

²⁵"Who are you?" they asked.

"Just what I have been claiming all along," Jesus replied. ²⁶"I have much to say in judgment of you. But he who sent me is reliable, and what I have heard from him I tell the world."

²⁷They did not understand that he was telling them about his Father. ²⁸So Jesus said, "When you have lifted up the Son of Man, then you will know that I am ˌthe one I claim to beˌ and that I do nothing on my own but speak just what the Father has taught me. ²⁹The one who sent me is with me; he has not left me alone, for I always do what pleases him." ³⁰Even as he spoke, many put their faith in him.

The Children of Abraham

³¹To the Jews who had believed him, Jesus said, "If you hold to my teaching, you are really my disciples. ³²Then you will know the truth, and the truth will set you free."

³³They answered him, "We are Abraham's descendants ᵇ and

ᵃ24 Or *I am he*; also in verse 28   ᵇ33 Greek *seed*; also in verse 37 have never been slaves of anyone. How can you say that we shall be set free?"

³⁴Jesus replied, "I tell you the truth, everyone who sins is a slave to sin. ³⁵Now a slave has no permanent place in the family, but a son belongs to it forever. ³⁶So if the Son sets you free, you will be free indeed. ³⁷I know you are Abraham's descendants. Yet you are ready to kill me, because you have no room for my word. ³⁸I am telling you what I have seen in the Father's presence, and you do what you have heard from your father. *ᵃ*"

³⁹"Abraham is our father," they answered.

"If you were Abraham's children," said Jesus, "then you would *ᵇ* do the things Abraham did. ⁴⁰As it is, you are determined to kill me, a man who has told you the truth that I heard from God. Abraham did not do such things. ⁴¹You are doing the things your own father does."

"We are not illegitimate children," they protested. "The only Father we have is God himself."

The Children of the Devil

⁴²Jesus said to them, "If God were your Father, you would love me, for I came from God and now am here. I have not come on my own; but he sent me. ⁴³Why is my language not clear to you? Because you are unable to hear what I say. ⁴⁴You belong to your father, the devil, and you want to carry out your father's desire. He was a murderer from the beginning, not holding to the truth, for there is no truth in him. When he lies, he speaks his native language, for he is a liar and the father of lies. ⁴⁵Yet because I tell the truth, you do not believe me! ⁴⁶Can any of you prove me guilty of sin? If I am telling the truth, why don't you believe me? ⁴⁷He who belongs to God hears what God says. The reason you do not hear is that you do not belong to God."

The Claims of Jesus About Himself

⁴⁸The Jews answered him, "Aren't we right in saying that you are a Samaritan and demon-possessed?"

⁴⁹"I am not possessed by a demon," said Jesus, "but I honor my Father and you dishonor me. ⁵⁰I am not seeking glory for myself; but there is one who seeks it, and he is the judge. ⁵¹I tell you the truth, if anyone keeps my word, he will never see death."

⁵²At this the Jews exclaimed, "Now we know that you are

ᵃ38 Or presence. Therefore do what you have heard from the Father.
ᵇ39 Some early manuscripts "If you are Abraham's children," said Jesus, "then

demon-possessed! Abraham died and so did the prophets, yet you say that if anyone keeps your word, he will never taste death. 53Are you greater than our father Abraham? He died, and so did the prophets. Who do you think you are?"

54Jesus replied, "If I glorify myself, my glory means nothing. My Father, whom you claim as your God, is the one who glorifies me. 55Though you do not know him, I know him. If I said I did not, I would be a liar like you, but I do know him and keep his word. 56Your father Abraham rejoiced at the thought of seeing my day; he saw it and was glad."

57"You are not yet fifty years old," the Jews said to him, "and you have seen Abraham!"

58"I tell you the truth," Jesus answered, "before Abraham was born, I am!" 59At this, they picked up stones to stone him, but Jesus hid himself, slipping away from the temple grounds.

Jesus Heals a Man Born Blind

9 As he went along, he saw a man blind from birth. 2His disciples asked him, "Rabbi, who sinned, this man or his parents, that he was born blind?"

3"Neither this man nor his parents sinned," said Jesus, "but this happened so that the work of God might be displayed in his life. 4As long as it is day, we must do the work of him who sent me. Night is coming, when no one can work. 5While I am in the world, I am the light of the world."

6Having said this, he spit on the ground, made some mud with the saliva, and put it on the man's eyes. 7"Go," he told him, "wash in the Pool of Siloam" (this word means Sent). So the man went and washed, and came home seeing.

8His neighbors and those who had formerly seen him begging asked, "Isn't this the same man who used to sit and beg?" 9Some claimed that he was.

Others said, "No, he only looks like him."

But he himself insisted, "I am the man."

10"How then were your eyes opened?" they demanded.

11He replied, "The man they call Jesus made some mud and put it on my eyes. He told me to go to Siloam and wash. So I went and washed, and then I could see."

12"Where is this man?" they asked him.

"I don't know," he said.

The Pharisees Investigate the Healing

13They brought to the Pharisees the man who had been blind.

14Now the day on which Jesus had made the mud and opened the man's eyes was a Sabbath. 15Therefore the Pharisees also asked him how he had received his sight. "He put mud on my eyes," the man replied, "and I washed, and now I see."

16Some of the Pharisees said, "This man is not from God, for he does not keep the Sabbath."

But others asked, "How can a sinner do such miraculous signs?" So they were divided.

17Finally they turned again to the blind man, "What have you to say about him? It was your eyes he opened."

The man replied, "He is a prophet."

18The Jews still did not believe that he had been blind and had received his sight until they sent for the man's parents. 19"Is this your son?" they asked. "Is this the one you say was born blind? How is it that now he can see?"

20"We know he is our son," the parents answered, "and we know he was born blind. 21But how he can see now, or who opened his eyes, we don't know. Ask him. He is of age; he will speak for himself." 22His parents said this because they were afraid of the Jews, for already the Jews had decided that anyone who acknowledged that Jesus was the Christ *a* would be put out of the synagogue. 23That was why his parents said, "He is of age; ask him."

24A second time they summoned the man who had been blind. "Give glory to God, *b*," they said. "We know this man is a sinner."

25He replied, "Whether he is a sinner or not, I don't know. One thing I do know. I was blind but now I see!"

26Then they asked him, "What did he do to you? How did he open your eyes?"

27He answered, "I have told you already and you did not listen. Why do you want to hear it again? Do you want to become his disciples, too?"

28Then they hurled insults at him and said, "You are this fellow's disciple! We are disciples of Moses! 29We know that God spoke to Moses, but as for this fellow, we don't even know where he comes from."

30The man answered, "Now that is remarkable! You don't know where he comes from, yet he opened my eyes. 31We know that God does not listen to sinners. He listens to the godly man who does his will. 32Nobody has ever heard of opening the eyes

a22 Or Messiah   *b24 A solemn charge to tell the truth (see Joshua 7:19)* of a man born blind. 33If this man were not from God, he could do nothing."

34To this they replied, "You were steeped in sin at birth; how dare you lecture us!" And they threw him out.

Spiritual Blindness

35Jesus heard that they had thrown him out, and when he found him, he said, "Do you believe in the Son of Man?"

36"Who is he, sir?" the man asked. "Tell me so that I may believe in him."

37Jesus said, "You have now seen him; in fact, he is the one speaking with you."

38Then the man said, "Lord, I believe," and he worshiped him.

39Jesus said, "For judgment I have come into this world, so that the blind will see and those who see will become blind."

40Some Pharisees who were with him heard him say this and asked, "What? Are we blind too?"

41Jesus said, "If you were blind, you would not be guilty of sin; but now that you claim you can see, your guilt remains.

The Shepherd and His Flock

10 "I tell you the truth, the man who does not enter the sheep pen by the gate, but climbs in by some other way, is a thief and a robber. 2The man who enters by the gate is the shepherd of his sheep. 3The watchman opens the gate for him, and the sheep listen to his voice. He calls his own sheep by name and leads them out. 4When he has brought out all his own, he goes on ahead of them, and his sheep follow him because they know his voice. 5But they will never follow a stranger; in fact, they will run away from him because they do not recognize a stranger's voice." 6Jesus used this figure of speech, but they did not understand what he was telling them.

7Therefore Jesus said again, "I tell you the truth, I am the gate for the sheep. 8All who ever came before me were thieves and robbers, but the sheep did not listen to them. 9I am the gate; whoever enters through me will be saved. a He will come in and go out, and find pasture. 10The thief comes only to steal and kill and destroy; I have come that they may have life, and have it to the full.

11"I am the good shepherd. The good shepherd lays down his life for the sheep. 12The hired hand is not the shepherd who

a9 Or kept safe

owns the sheep. So when he sees the wolf coming, he abandons the sheep and runs away. Then the wolf attacks the flock and scatters it. [13]The man runs away because he is a hired hand and cares nothing for the sheep.

[14]"I am the good shepherd; I know my sheep and my sheep know me— [15]just as the Father knows me and I know the Father—and I lay down my life for the sheep. [16]I have other sheep that are not of this sheep pen. I must bring them also. They too will listen to my voice, and there shall be one flock and one shepherd. [17]The reason my Father loves me is that I lay down my life—only to take it up again. [18]No one takes it from me, but I lay it down of my own accord. I have authority to lay it down and authority to take it up again. This command I received from my Father."

[19]At these words the Jews were again divided. [20]Many of them said, "He is demon-possessed and raving mad. Why listen to him?"

[21]But others said, "These are not the sayings of a man possessed by a demon. Can a demon open the eyes of the blind?"

The Unbelief of the Jews

[22]Then came the Feast of Dedication *a* at Jerusalem. It was winter, [23]and Jesus was in the temple area walking in Solomon's Colonnade. [24]The Jews gathered around him, saying, "How long will you keep us in suspense? If you are the Christ, *b* tell us plainly."

[25]Jesus answered, "I did tell you, but you do not believe. The miracles I do in my Father's name speak for me, [26]but you do not believe because you are not my sheep. [27]My sheep listen to my voice; I know them, and they follow me. [28]I give them eternal life, and they shall never perish; no one can snatch them out of my hand. [29]My Father, who has given them to me, is greater than all *c*; no one can snatch them out of my Father's hand. [30]I and the Father are one."

[31]Again the Jews picked up stones to stone him, [32]but Jesus said to them, "I have shown you many great miracles from the Father. For which of these do you stone me?"

[33]"We are not stoning you for any of these," replied the Jews, "but for blasphemy, because you, a mere man, claim to be God."

---

a22 That is, Hanukkah   *b24* Or *Messiah*   *c29* Many early manuscripts
What my Father has given me is greater than all

³⁴Jesus answered them, "Is it not written in your Law, 'I have said you are gods' ᵃ? ³⁵If he called them 'gods,' to whom the word of God came—and the Scripture cannot be broken—³⁶what about the one whom the Father set apart as his very own and sent into the world? Why then do you accuse me of blasphemy because I said, 'I am God's Son'? ³⁷Do not believe me unless I do what my Father does. ³⁸But if I do it, even though you do not believe me, believe the miracles, that you may know and understand that the Father is in me, and I in the Father." ³⁹Again they tried to seize him, but he escaped their grasp.

⁴⁰Then Jesus went back across the Jordan to the place where John had been baptizing in the early days. Here he stayed ⁴¹and many people came to him. They said, "Though John never performed a miraculous sign, all that John said about this man was true." ⁴²And in that place many believed in Jesus.

The Death of Lazarus

11 Now a man named Lazarus was sick. He was from Bethany, the village of Mary and her sister Martha. ²This Mary, whose brother Lazarus now lay sick, was the same one who poured perfume on the Lord and wiped his feet with her hair. ³So the sisters sent word to Jesus, "Lord, the one you love is sick."

⁴When he heard this, Jesus said, "This sickness will not end in death. No, it is for God's glory so that God's Son may be glorified through it." ⁵Jesus loved Martha and her sister and Lazarus. ⁶Yet when he heard that Lazarus was sick, he stayed where he was two more days.

⁷Then he said to his disciples, "Let us go back to Judea."

⁸"But Rabbi," they said, "a short while ago the Jews tried to stone you, and yet you are going back there?"

⁹Jesus answered, "Are there not twelve hours of daylight? A man who walks by day will not stumble, for he sees by this world's light. ¹⁰It is when he walks by night that he stumbles, for he has no light."

¹¹After he had said this, he went on to tell them, "Our friend Lazarus has fallen asleep; but I am going there to wake him up."

¹²His disciples replied, "Lord, if he sleeps, he will get better." ¹³Jesus had been speaking of his death, but his disciples thought he meant natural sleep.

ᵃ34 Psalm 82:6

[14]So then he told them plainly, "Lazarus is dead, [15]and for your sake I am glad I was not there, so that you may believe. But let us go to him."

[16]Then Thomas (called Didymus) said to the rest of the disciples, "Let us also go, that we may die with him."

Jesus Comforts the Sisters

[17]On his arrival, Jesus found that Lazarus had already been in the tomb for four days. [18]Bethany was less than two miles *a* from Jerusalem, [19]and many Jews had come to Martha and Mary to comfort them in the loss of their brother. [20]When Martha heard that Jesus was coming, she went out to meet him, but Mary stayed at home.

[21]"Lord," Martha said to Jesus, "if you had been here, my brother would not have died. [22]But I know that even now God will give you whatever you ask."

[23]Jesus said to her, "Your brother will rise again."

[24]Martha answered, "I know he will rise again in the resurrection at the last day."

[25]Jesus said to her, "I am the resurrection and the life. He who believes in me will live, even though he dies; [26]and whoever lives and believes in me will never die. Do you believe this?"

[27]"Yes, Lord," she told him, "I believe that you are the Christ, *b* the Son of God, who was to come into the world."

[28]And after she had said this, she went back and called her sister Mary aside. "The Teacher is here," she said, "and is asking for you." [29]When Mary heard this, she got up quickly and went to him. [30]Now Jesus had not yet entered the village, but was still at the place where Martha had met him. [31]When the Jews who had been with Mary in the house, comforting her, noticed how quickly she got up and went out, they followed her, supposing she was going to the tomb to mourn there.

[32]When Mary reached the place where Jesus was and saw him, she fell at his feet and said, "Lord, if you had been here, my brother would not have died."

[33]When Jesus saw her weeping, and the Jews who had come along with her also weeping, he was deeply moved in spirit and troubled. [34]"Where have you laid him?" he asked.

"Come and see, Lord," they replied.

[35]Jesus wept.

[36]Then the Jews said, "See how he loved him!"

a18 Greek *fifteen stadia* (about 3 kilometers)   *b27* Or *Messiah*

37But some of them said, "Could not he who opened the eyes of the blind man have kept this man from dying?"

Jesus Raises Lazarus From the Dead

38Jesus, once more deeply moved, came to the tomb. It was a cave with a stone laid across the entrance. 39"Take away the stone," he said.

"But, Lord," said Martha, the sister of the dead man, "by this time there is a bad odor, for he has been there four days."

40Then Jesus said, "Did I not tell you that if you believed, you would see the glory of God?"

41So they took away the stone. Then Jesus looked up and said, "Father, I thank you that you have heard me. 42I knew that you always hear me, but I said this for the benefit of the people standing here, that they may believe that you sent me."

43When he had said this, Jesus called in a loud voice, "Lazarus, come out!" 44The dead man came out, his hands and feet wrapped with strips of linen, and a cloth around his face.

Jesus said to them, "Take off the grave clothes and let him go."

The Plot to Kill Jesus

45Therefore many of the Jews who had come to visit Mary, and had seen what Jesus did, put their faith in him. 46But some of them went to the Pharisees and told them what Jesus had done. 47Then the chief priests and the Pharisees called a meeting of the Sanhedrin.

"What are we accomplishing?" they asked. "Here is this man performing many miraculous signs. 48If we let him go on like this, everyone will believe in him, and then the Romans will come and take away both our place *a* and our nation."

49Then one of them, named Caiaphas, who was high priest that year, spoke up, "You know nothing at all! 50You do not realize that it is better for you that one man die for the people than that the whole nation perish."

51He did not say this on his own, but as high priest that year he prophesied that Jesus would die for the Jewish nation, 52and not only for that nation but also for the scattered children of God, to bring them together and make them one. 53So from that day on they plotted to take his life.

54Therefore Jesus no longer moved about publicly among the

a48 Or temple

Jews. Instead he withdrew to a region near the desert, to a village called Ephraim, where he stayed with his disciples.

55When it was almost time for the Jewish Passover, many went up from the country to Jerusalem for their ceremonial cleansing before the Passover. 56They kept looking for Jesus, and as they stood in the temple area they asked one another, "What do you think? Isn't he coming to the Feast at all?" 57But the chief priests and Pharisees had given orders that if anyone found out where Jesus was, he should report it so that they might arrest him.

Jesus Anointed at Bethany

12 Six days before the Passover, Jesus arrived at Bethany, where Lazarus lived, whom Jesus had raised from the dead. 2Here a dinner was given in Jesus' honor. Martha served, while Lazarus was among those reclining at the table with him. 3Then Mary took about a pint *a* of pure nard, an expensive perfume; she poured it on Jesus' feet and wiped his feet with her hair. And the house was filled with the fragrance of the perfume.

4But one of his disciples, Judas Iscariot, who was later to betray him, objected, 5"Why wasn't this perfume sold and the money given to the poor? It was worth a year's wages. *b*" 6He did not say this because he cared about the poor but because he was a thief; as keeper of the money bag, he used to help himself to what was put into it.

7"Leave her alone," Jesus replied. "It was intended that she should save this perfume for the day of my burial. 8You will always have the poor among you, but you will not always have me."

9Meanwhile a large crowd of Jews found out that Jesus was there and came, not only because of him but also to see Lazarus, whom he had raised from the dead. 10So the chief priests made plans to kill Lazarus as well, 11for on account of him many of the Jews were going over to Jesus and putting their faith in him.

The Triumphal Entry

12The next day the great crowd that had come for the Feast heard that Jesus was on his way to Jerusalem. 13They took palm branches and went out to meet him, shouting,

a3 Greek *a litra* (probably about 0.5 liter)   *b5* Greek *three hundred denarii*

"Hosanna! *a*"

"Blessed is he who comes in the name of the
     Lord!" *b*

"Blessed is the King of Israel!"

14Jesus found a young donkey and sat upon it, as it is written,

15"Do not be afraid, O Daughter of Zion;
     see, your king is coming,
     seated on a donkey's colt." *c*

16At first his disciples did not understand all this. Only after Jesus was glorified did they realize that these things had been written about him and that they had done these things to him. 17Now the crowd that was with him when he called Lazarus from the tomb and raised him from the dead continued to spread the word. 18Many people, because they had heard that he had given this miraculous sign, went out to meet him. 19So the Pharisees said to one another, "See, this is getting us nowhere. Look how the whole world has gone after him!"

Jesus Predicts His Death

20Now there were some Greeks among those who went up to worship at the Feast. 21They came to Philip, who was from Bethsaida in Galilee, with a request. "Sir," they said, "we would like to see Jesus." 22Philip went to tell Andrew; Andrew and Philip in turn told Jesus.

23Jesus replied, "The hour has come for the Son of Man to be glorified. 24I tell you the truth, unless a kernel of wheat falls to the ground and dies, it remains only a single seed. But if it dies, it produces many seeds. 25The man who loves his life will lose it, while the man who hates his life in this world will keep it for eternal life. 26Whoever serves me must follow me; and where I am, my servant also will be. My Father will honor the one who serves me.

27"Now my heart is troubled, and what shall I say? 'Father, save me from this hour'? No, it was for this very reason I came to this hour. 28Father, glorify your name!"

Then a voice came from heaven, "I have glorified it, and will glorify it again." 29The crowd that was there and heard it said it had thundered; others said an angel had spoken to him.

a13 A Hebrew expression meaning "Save!" which became an exclamation of praise   *b13* Psalm 118:25, 26   *c15* Zech. 9:9

³⁰Jesus said, "This voice was for your benefit, not mine. ³¹Now is the time for judgment on this world; now the prince of this world will be driven out. ³²But I, when I am lifted up from the earth, will draw all men to myself." ³³He said this to show the kind of death he was going to die.

³⁴The crowd spoke up, "We have heard from the Law that the Christ ᵃ will remain forever, so how can you say, 'The Son of Man must be lifted up'? Who is this 'Son of Man'?"

³⁵Then Jesus told them, "You are going to have the light just a little while longer. Walk while you have the light, before darkness overtakes you. The man who walks in the dark does not know where he is going. ³⁶Put your trust in the light while you have it, so that you may become sons of light." When he had finished speaking, Jesus left and hid himself from them.

The Jews Continue in Their Unbelief

³⁷Even after Jesus had done all these miraculous signs in their presence, they still would not believe in him. ³⁸This was to fulfill the word of Isaiah the prophet:

> "Lord, who has believed our message
> and to whom has the arm of the Lord been
> revealed?" ᵇ

³⁹For this reason they could not believe, because, as Isaiah says elsewhere:

> ⁴⁰"He has blinded their eyes
> and deadened their hearts,
> so they can neither see with their eyes,
> nor understand with their hearts,
> nor turn—and I would heal them." ᶜ

⁴¹Isaiah said this because he saw Jesus' glory and spoke about him.

⁴²Yet at the same time many even among the leaders believed in him. But because of the Pharisees they would not confess their faith for fear they would be put out of the synagogue; ⁴³for they loved praise from men more than praise from God.

⁴⁴Then Jesus cried out, "When a man believes in me, he does not believe in me only, but in the one who sent me. ⁴⁵When he looks at me, he sees the one who sent me. ⁴⁶I have come into

---

ᵃ34 Or *Messiah*   ᵇ38 Isaiah 53:1   ᶜ40 Isaiah 6:10

the world as a light, so that no one who believes in me should stay in darkness.

47"As for the person who hears my words but does not keep them, I do not judge him. For I did not come to judge the world, but to save it. 48There is a judge for the one who rejects me and does not accept my words; that very word which I spoke will condemn him at the last day. 49For I did not speak of my own accord, but the Father who sent me commanded me what to say and how to say it. 50I know that his command leads to eternal life. So whatever I say is just what the Father has told me to say."

Jesus Washes His Disciples' Feet

13 It was just before the Passover Feast. Jesus knew that the time had come for him to leave this world and go to the Father. Having loved his own who were in the world, he now showed them the full extent of his love. *a*

2The evening meal was being served, and the devil had already prompted Judas Iscariot, son of Simon, to betray Jesus. 3Jesus knew that the Father had put all things under his power, and that he had come from God and was returning to God; 4so he got up from the meal, took off his outer clothing, and wrapped a towel around his waist. 5After that, he poured water into a basin and began to wash his disciples' feet, drying them with the towel that was wrapped around him.

6He came to Simon Peter, who said to him, "Lord, are you going to wash my feet?"

7Jesus replied, "You do not realize now what I am doing, but later you will understand."

8"No," said Peter, "you shall never wash my feet."

Jesus answered, "Unless I wash you, you have no part with me."

9"Then, Lord," Simon Peter replied, "not just my feet but my hands and my head as well!"

10Jesus answered, "A person who has had a bath needs only to wash his feet; his whole body is clean. And you are clean, though not every one of you." 11For he knew who was going to betray him, and that was why he said not every one was clean.

12When he had finished washing their feet, he put on his clothes and returned to his place. "Do you understand what I have done for you?" he asked them. 13"You call me 'Teacher' and 'Lord,' and rightly so, for that is what I am. 14Now that I, your

a1 Or he loved them to the last

Lord and Teacher, have washed your feet, you also should wash one another's feet. [15]I have set you an example that you should do as I have done for you. [16]I tell you the truth, no servant is greater than his master, nor is a messenger greater than the one who sent him. [17]Now that you know these things, you will be blessed if you do them.

Jesus Predicts His Betrayal

[18]"I am not referring to all of you; I know those I have chosen. But this is to fulfill the scripture: 'He who shares my bread has lifted up his heel against me.' [a]

[19]"I am telling you now before it happens, so that when it does happen you will believe that I am He. [20]I tell you the truth, whoever accepts anyone I send accepts me; and whoever accepts me accepts the one who sent me."

[21]After he had said this, Jesus was troubled in spirit and testified, "I tell you the truth, one of you is going to betray me."

[22]His disciples stared at one another, at a loss to know which of them he meant. [23]One of them, the disciple whom Jesus loved, was reclining next to him. [24]Simon Peter motioned to this disciple and said, "Ask him which one he means."

[25]Leaning back against Jesus, he asked him, "Lord, who is it?"

[26]Jesus answered, "It is the one to whom I will give this piece of bread when I have dipped it in the dish." Then, dipping the piece of bread, he gave it to Judas Iscariot, son of Simon. [27]As soon as Judas took the bread, Satan entered into him.

"What you are about to do, do quickly," Jesus told him, [28]but no one at the meal understood why Jesus said this to him. [29]Since Judas had charge of the money, some thought Jesus was telling him to buy what was needed for the Feast, or to give something to the poor. [30]As soon as Judas had taken the bread, he went out. And it was night.

Jesus Predicts Peter's Denial

[31]When he was gone, Jesus said, "Now is the Son of Man glorified and God is glorified in him. [32]If God is glorified in him, [b] God will glorify the Son in himself, and will glorify him at once.

[33]"My children, I will be with you only a little longer. You will

---

a18 Psalm 41:9   *b32* Many early manuscripts do not have *If God is glorified in him.*

look for me, and just as I told the Jews, so I tell you now: Where I am going, you cannot come.

34"A new command I give you: Love one another. As I have loved you, so you must love one another. 35By this all men will know that you are my disciples, if you love one another."

36Simon Peter asked him, "Lord, where are you going?"

Jesus replied, "Where I am going, you cannot follow now, but you will follow later."

37Peter asked, "Lord, why can't I follow you now? I will lay down my life for you."

38Then Jesus answered, "Will you really lay down your life for me? I tell you the truth, before the rooster crows, you will disown me three times!

Jesus Comforts His Disciples

14 "Do not let your hearts be troubled. Trust in God *a*; trust also in me. 2In my Father's house are many rooms; if it were not so, I would have told you. I am going there to prepare a place for you. 3And if I go and prepare a place for you, I will come back and take you to be with me that you also may be where I am. 4You know the way to the place where I am going."

Jesus the Way to the Father

5Thomas said to him, "Lord, we don't know where you are going, so how can we know the way?"

6Jesus answered, "I am the way and the truth and the life. No one comes to the Father except through me. 7If you really knew me, you would know *b* my Father as well. From now on, you do know him and have seen him."

8Philip said, "Lord, show us the Father and that will be enough for us."

9Jesus answered: "Don't you know me, Philip, even after I have been among you such a long time? Anyone who has seen me has seen the Father. How can you say, 'Show us the Father'? 10Don't you believe that I am in the Father, and that the Father is in me? The words I say to you are not just my own. Rather, it is the Father, living in me, who is doing his work. 11Believe me when I say that I am in the Father and the Father is in me; or at least believe on the evidence of the miracles themselves. 12I tell you the truth, anyone who has faith in me will

a1 Or You trust in God   b7 Some early manuscripts If you really have known me, you will know

do what I have been doing. He will do even greater things than these, because I am going to the Father. [13]And I will do whatever you ask in my name, so that the Son may bring glory to the Father. [14]You may ask me for anything in my name, and I will do it.

Jesus Promises the Holy Spirit

[15]"If you love me, you will obey what I command. [16]And I will ask the Father, and he will give you another Counselor to be with you forever— [17]the Spirit of truth. The world cannot accept him, because it neither sees him nor knows him. But you know him, for he lives with you and will be *a* in you. [18]I will not leave you as orphans; I will come to you. [19]Before long, the world will not see me anymore, but you will see me. Because I live, you also will live. [20]On that day you will realize that I am in my Father, and you are in me, and I am in you. [21]Whoever has my commands and obeys them, he is the one who loves me. He who loves me will be loved by my Father, and I too will love him and show myself to him."

[22]Then Judas (not Judas Iscariot) said, "But, Lord, why do you intend to show yourself to us and not to the world?"

[23]Jesus replied, "If anyone loves me, he will obey my teaching. My Father will love him, and we will come to him and make our home with him. [24]He who does not love me will not obey my teaching. These words you hear are not my own; they belong to the Father who sent me.

[25]"All this I have spoken while still with you. [26]But the Counselor, the Holy Spirit, whom the Father will send in my name, will teach you all things and will remind you of everything I have said to you. [27]Peace I leave with you; my peace I give you. I do not give to you as the world gives. Do not let your hearts be troubled and do not be afraid.

[28]"You heard me say, 'I am going away and I am coming back to you.' If you loved me, you would be glad that I am going to the Father, for the Father is greater than I. [29]I have told you now before it happens, so that when it does happen you will believe. [30]I will not speak with you much longer, for the prince of this world is coming. He has no hold on me, [31]but the world must learn that I love the Father and that I do exactly what my Father has commanded me.

"Come now; let us leave.

a17 Some early manuscripts *and is*

The Vine and the Branches

15 "I am the true vine, and my Father is the gardener. 2He cuts off every branch in me that bears no fruit, while every branch that does bear fruit he prunes *a* so that it will be even more fruitful. 3You are already clean because of the word I have spoken to you. 4Remain in me, and I will remain in you. No branch can bear fruit by itself; it must remain in the vine. Neither can you bear fruit unless you remain in me.

5"I am the vine; you are the branches. If a man remains in me and I in him, he will bear much fruit; apart from me you can do nothing. 6If anyone does not remain in me, he is like a branch that is thrown away and withers; such branches are picked up, thrown into the fire and burned. 7If you remain in me and my words remain in you, ask whatever you wish, and it will be given you. 8This is to my Father's glory, that you bear much fruit, showing yourselves to be my disciples.

9"As the Father has loved me, so have I loved you. Now remain in my love. 10If you obey my commands, you will remain in my love, just as I have obeyed my Father's commands and remain in his love. 11I have told you this so that my joy may be in you and that your joy may be complete. 12My command is this: Love each other as I have loved you. 13Greater love has no one than this, that he lay down his life for his friends. 14You are my friends if you do what I command. 15I no longer call you servants, because a servant does not know his master's business. Instead, I have called you friends, for everything that I learned from my Father I have made known to you. 16You did not choose me, but I chose you and appointed you to go and bear fruit—fruit that will last. Then the Father will give you whatever you ask in my name. 17This is my command: Love each other.

The World Hates the Disciples

18"If the world hates you, keep in mind that it hated me first. 19If you belonged to the world, it would love you as its own. As it is, you do not belong to the world, but I have chosen you out of the world. That is why the world hates you. 20Remember the words I spoke to you: 'No servant is greater than his master.' *b* If they persecuted me, they will persecute you also. If they obeyed my teaching, they will obey yours also. 21They will treat you this way because of my name, for they do not know the One who sent me. 22If I had not come and spoken to them, they would

a2 The Greek for *prunes* also means *cleans.*   *b20* John 13:16

not be guilty of sin. Now, however, they have no excuse for their sin. 23He who hates me hates my Father as well. 24If I had not done among them what no one else did, they would not be guilty of sin. But now they have seen these miracles, and yet they have hated both me and my Father. 25But this is to fulfill what is written in their Law: 'They hated me without reason.' *a*

26"When the Counselor comes, whom I will send to you from the Father, the Spirit of truth who goes out from the Father, he will testify about me. 27And you also must testify, for you have been with me from the beginning.

16 "All this I have told you so that you will not go astray. 2They will put you out of the synagogue; in fact, a time is coming when anyone who kills you will think he is offering a service to God. 3They will do such things because they have not known the Father or me. 4I have told you this, so that when the time comes you will remember that I warned you. I did not tell you this at first because I was with you.

The Work of the Holy Spirit

5"Now I am going to him who sent me, yet none of you asks me, 'Where are you going?' 6Because I have said these things, you are filled with grief. 7But I tell you the truth: It is for your good that I am going away. Unless I go away, the Counselor will not come to you; but if I go, I will send him to you. 8When he comes, he will convict the world of guilt *b* in regard to sin and righteousness and judgment: 9in regard to sin, because men do not believe in me; 10in regard to righteousness, because I am going to the Father, where you can see me no longer; 11and in regard to judgment, because the prince of this world now stands condemned.

12"I have much more to say to you, more than you can now bear. 13But when he, the Spirit of truth, comes, he will guide you into all truth. He will not speak on his own; he will speak only what he hears, and he will tell you what is yet to come. 14He will bring glory to me by taking from what is mine and making it known to you. 15All that belongs to the Father is mine. That is why I said the Spirit will take from what is mine and make it known to you.

16"In a little while you will see me no more, and then after a little while you will see me."

---

*a*25 Psalms 35:19; 69:4   *b*8 Or *will expose the guilt of the world*

The Disciples' Grief Will Turn to Joy

17Some of his disciples said to one another, "What does he mean by saying, 'In a little while you will see me no more, and then after a little while you will see me,' and 'Because I am going to the Father'?" 18They kept asking, "What does he mean by 'a little while'? We don't understand what he is saying."

19Jesus saw that they wanted to ask him about this, so he said to them, "Are you asking one another what I meant when I said, 'In a little while you will see me no more, and then after a little while you will see me'? 20I tell you the truth, you will weep and mourn while the world rejoices. You will grieve, but your grief will turn to joy. 21A woman giving birth to a child has pain because her time has come; but when her baby is born she forgets the anguish because of her joy that a child is born into the world. 22So with you: Now is your time of grief, but I will see you again and you will rejoice, and no one will take away your joy. 23In that day you will no longer ask me anything. I tell you the truth, my Father will give you whatever you ask in my name. 24Until now you have not asked for anything in my name. Ask and you will receive, and your joy will be complete.

25"Though I have been speaking figuratively, a time is coming when I will no longer use this kind of language but will tell you plainly about my Father. 26In that day you will ask in my name. I am not saying that I will ask the Father on your behalf. 27No, the Father himself loves you because you have loved me and have believed that I came from God. 28I came from the Father and entered the world; now I am leaving the world and going back to the Father."

29Then Jesus' disciples said, "Now you are speaking clearly and without figures of speech. 30Now we can see that you know all things and that you do not even need to have anyone ask you questions. This makes us believe that you came from God."

31"You believe at last!" *a* Jesus answered. 32"But a time is coming, and has come, when you will be scattered, each to his own home. You will leave me all alone. Yet I am not alone, for my Father is with me.

33"I have told you these things, so that in me you may have peace. In this world you will have trouble. But take heart! I have overcome the world."

a31 Or "Do you now believe?"

Jesus Prays for Himself

17 After Jesus said this, he looked toward heaven and prayed:

"Father, the time has come. Glorify your Son, that your Son may glorify you. ²For you granted him authority over all people that he might give eternal life to all those you have given him. ³Now this is eternal life: that they may know you, the only true God, and Jesus Christ, whom you have sent. ⁴I have brought you glory on earth by completing the work you gave me to do. ⁵And now, Father, glorify me in your presence with the glory I had with you before the world began.

Jesus Prays for His Disciples

⁶"I have revealed you ᵃ to those whom you gave me out of the world. They were yours; you gave them to me and they have obeyed your word. ⁷Now they know that everything you have given me comes from you. ⁸For I gave them the words you gave me and they accepted them. They knew with certainty that I came from you, and they believed that you sent me. ⁹I pray for them. I am not praying for the world, but for those you have given me, for they are yours. ¹⁰All I have is yours, and all you have is mine. And glory has come to me through them. ¹¹I will remain in the world no longer, but they are still in the world, and I am coming to you. Holy Father, protect them by the power of your name— the name you gave me—so that they may be one as we are one. ¹²While I was with them, I protected them and kept them safe by that name you gave me. None has been lost except the one doomed to destruction so that Scripture would be fulfilled.

¹³"I am coming to you now, but I say these things while I am still in the world, so that they may have the full measure of my joy within them. ¹⁴I have given them your word and the world has hated them, for they are not of the world any more than I am of the world. ¹⁵My prayer is not that you take them out of the world but that you protect them from the evil one. ¹⁶They are not of the world, even as I am not of it. ¹⁷Sanctify ᵇ them by the truth; your word is truth. ¹⁸As you

---

ᵃ6 Greek *your name;* also in verse 26   ᵇ17 Greek *hagiazo (set apart for sacred use or make holy);* also in verse 19

sent me into the world, I have sent them into the world. ¹⁹For them I sanctify myself, that they too may be truly sanctified.

Jesus Prays for All Believers

²⁰"My prayer is not for them alone. I pray also for those who will believe in me through their message, ²¹that all of them may be one, Father, just as you are in me and I am in you. May they also be in us so that the world may believe that you have sent me. ²²I have given them the glory that you gave me, that they may be one as we are one: ²³I in them and you in me. May they be brought to complete unity to let the world know that you sent me and have loved them even as you have loved me.

²⁴"Father, I want those you have given me to be with me where I am, and to see my glory, the glory you have given me because you loved me before the creation of the world.

²⁵"Righteous Father, though the world does not know you, I know you, and they know that you have sent me. ²⁶I have made you known to them, and will continue to make you known in order that the love you have for me may be in them and that I myself may be in them."

Jesus Arrested

18 When he had finished praying, Jesus left with his disciples and crossed the Kidron Valley. On the other side there was an olive grove, and he and his disciples went into it.

²Now Judas, who betrayed him, knew the place, because Jesus had often met there with his disciples. ³So Judas came to the grove, guiding a detachment of soldiers and some officials from the chief priests and Pharisees. They were carrying torches, lanterns and weapons.

⁴Jesus, knowing all that was going to happen to him, went out and asked them, "Who is it you want?"

⁵"Jesus of Nazareth," they replied.

"I am he," Jesus said. (And Judas the traitor was standing there with them.) ⁶When Jesus said, "I am he," they drew back and fell to the ground.

⁷Again he asked them, "Who is it you want?"

And they said, "Jesus of Nazareth."

⁸"I told you that I am he," Jesus answered. "If you are looking for me, then let these men go." ⁹This happened so that the

words he had spoken would be fulfilled: "I have not lost one of those you gave me." *a*

¹⁰Then Simon Peter, who had a sword, drew it and struck the high priest's servant, cutting off his right ear. (The servant's name was Malchus.)

¹¹Jesus commanded Peter, "Put your sword away! Shall I not drink the cup the Father has given me?"

Jesus Taken to Annas

¹²Then the detachment of soldiers with its commander and the Jewish officials arrested Jesus. They bound him ¹³and brought him first to Annas, who was the father-in-law of Caiaphas, the high priest that year. ¹⁴Caiaphas was the one who had advised the Jews that it would be good if one man died for the people.

Peter's First Denial

¹⁵Simon Peter and another disciple were following Jesus. Because this disciple was known to the high priest, he went with Jesus into the high priest's courtyard, ¹⁶but Peter had to wait outside at the door. The other disciple, who was known to the high priest, came back, spoke to the girl on duty there and brought Peter in.

¹⁷"You are not one of his disciples, are you?" the girl at the door asked Peter.

He replied, "I am not."

¹⁸It was cold, and the servants and officials stood around a fire they had made to keep warm. Peter also was standing with them, warming himself.

The High Priest Questions Jesus

¹⁹Meanwhile, the high priest questioned Jesus about his disciples and his teaching.

²⁰"I have spoken openly to the world," Jesus replied. "I always taught in synagogues or at the temple, where all the Jews come together. I said nothing in secret. ²¹Why question me? Ask those who heard me. Surely they know what I said."

²²When Jesus said this, one of the officials nearby struck him in the face. "Is this the way you answer the high priest?" he demanded.

²³"If I said something wrong," Jesus replied, "testify as to

*a*9 John 6:39

what is wrong. But if I spoke the truth, why did you strike me?" [24]Then Annas sent him, still bound, to Caiaphas the high priest. *a*

Peter's Second and Third Denials

[25]As Simon Peter stood warming himself, he was asked, "You are not one of his disciples, are you?"

He denied it, saying, "I am not."

[26]One of the high priest's servants, a relative of the man whose ear Peter had cut off, challenged him, "Didn't I see you with him in the olive grove?" [27]Again Peter denied it, and at that moment a rooster began to crow.

Jesus Before Pilate

[28]Then the Jews led Jesus from Caiaphas to the palace of the Roman governor. By now it was early morning, and to avoid ceremonial uncleanness the Jews did not enter the palace; they wanted to be able to eat the Passover. [29]So Pilate came out to them and asked, "What charges are you bringing against this man?"

[30]"If he were not a criminal," they replied, "we would not have handed him over to you."

[31]Pilate said, "Take him yourselves and judge him by your own law."

"But we have no right to execute anyone," the Jews objected. [32]This happened so that the words Jesus had spoken indicating the kind of death he was going to die would be fulfilled.

[33]Pilate then went back inside the palace, summoned Jesus and asked him, "Are you the king of the Jews?"

[34]"Is that your own idea," Jesus asked, "or did others talk to you about me?"

[35]"Am I a Jew?" Pilate replied. "It was your people and your chief priests who handed you over to me. What is it you have done?"

[36]Jesus said, "My kingdom is not of this world. If it were, my servants would fight to prevent my arrest by the Jews. But now my kingdom is from another place."

[37]"You are a king, then!" said Pilate.

Jesus answered, "You are right in saying I am a king. In fact, for this reason I was born, and for this I came into the world, to testify to the truth. Everyone on the side of truth listens to me."

[38]"What is truth?" Pilate asked. With this he went out again

---

*a*24 Or *(Now Annas had sent him, still bound, to Caiaphas the high priest.)*

to the Jews and said, "I find no basis for a charge against him. ³⁹But it is your custom for me to release to you one prisoner at the time of the Passover. Do you want me to release 'the king of the Jews'?"

⁴⁰They shouted back, "No, not him! Give us Barabbas!" Now Barabbas had taken part in a rebellion.

Jesus Sentenced to be Crucified

19 Then Pilate took Jesus and had him flogged. ²The soldiers twisted together a crown of thorns and put it on his head. They clothed him in a purple robe ³and went up to him again and again, saying, "Hail, king of the Jews!" And they struck him in the face.

⁴Once more Pilate came out and said to the Jews, "Look, I am bringing him out to you to let you know that I find no basis for a charge against him." ⁵When Jesus came out wearing the crown of thorns and the purple robe, Pilate said to them, "Here is the man!"

⁶As soon as the chief priests and their officials saw him, they shouted, "Crucify! Crucify!"

But Pilate answered, "You take him and crucify him. As for me, I find no basis for a charge against him."

⁷The Jews insisted, "We have a law, and according to that law he must die, because he claimed to be the Son of God."

⁸When Pilate heard this, he was even more afraid, ⁹and he went back inside the palace. "Where do you come from?" he asked Jesus, but Jesus gave him no answer. ¹⁰"Do you refuse to speak to me?" Pilate said. "Don't you realize I have power either to free you or to crucify you?"

¹¹Jesus answered, "You would have no power over me if it were not given to you from above. Therefore the one who handed me over to you is guilty of a greater sin."

¹²From then on, Pilate tried to set Jesus free, but the Jews kept shouting, "If you let this man go, you are no friend of Caesar. Anyone who claims to be a king opposes Caesar."

¹³When Pilate heard this, he brought Jesus out and sat down on the judge's seat at a place known as the Stone Pavement (which in Aramaic is Gabbatha). ¹⁴It was the day of Preparation of Passover Week, about the sixth hour.

"Here is your king," Pilate said to the Jews.

¹⁵But they shouted, "Take him away! Take him away! Crucify him!"

"Shall I crucify your king?" Pilate asked.

"We have no king but Caesar," the chief priests answered.
¹⁶Finally Pilate handed him over to them to be crucified.

The Crucifixion

So the soldiers took charge of Jesus. ¹⁷Carrying his own
cross, he went out to the place of the Skull (which in Aramaic
is called Golgotha). ¹⁸Here they crucified him, and with him two
others—one on each side and Jesus in the middle.

¹⁹Pilate had a notice prepared and fastened to the cross. It
read: JESUS OF NAZARETH, THE KING OF THE JEWS. ²⁰Many of the Jews
read this sign, for the place where Jesus was crucified was near
the city, and the sign was written in Aramaic, Latin and Greek.
²¹The chief priests of the Jews protested to Pilate, "Do not write
'The King of the Jews,' but that this man claimed to be king of
the Jews."

²²Pilate answered, "What I have written, I have written."

²³When the soldiers crucified Jesus, they took his clothes,
dividing them into four shares, one for each of them, with the
undergarment remaining. This garment was seamless, woven
in one piece from top to bottom.

²⁴"Let's not tear it," they said to one another. "Let's decide by
lot who will get it."

This happened that the scripture might be fulfilled which said,

> "They divided my garments among them
>   and cast lots for my clothing." ᵃ

So this is what the soldiers did.

²⁵Near the cross of Jesus stood his mother, his mother's
sister, Mary the wife of Clopas, and Mary Magdalene. ²⁶When
Jesus saw his mother there, and the disciple whom he loved
standing nearby, he said to his mother, "Dear woman, here is
your son," ²⁷and to the disciple, "Here is your mother." From that
time on, this disciple took her into his home.

The Death of Jesus

²⁸Later, knowing that all was now completed, and so that the
Scripture would be fulfilled, Jesus said, "I am thirsty." ²⁹A jar of
wine vinegar was there, so they soaked a sponge in it, put the
sponge on a stalk of the hyssop plant, and lifted it to Jesus' lips.
³⁰When he had received the drink, Jesus said, "It is finished."
With that, he bowed his head and gave up his spirit.

ᵃ24 Psalm 22:18

³¹Now it was the day of Preparation, and the next day was to be a special Sabbath. Because the Jews did not want the bodies left on the crosses during the Sabbath, they asked Pilate to have the legs broken and the bodies taken down. ³²The soldiers therefore came and broke the legs of the first man who had been crucified with Jesus, and then those of the other. ³³But when they came to Jesus and found that he was already dead, they did not break his legs. ³⁴Instead, one of the soldiers pierced Jesus' side with a spear, bringing a sudden flow of blood and water. ³⁵The man who saw it has given testimony, and his testimony is true. He knows that he tells the truth, and he testifies so that you also may believe. ³⁶These things happened so that the scripture would be fulfilled: "Not one of his bones will be broken," ª ³⁷and, as another scripture says, "They will look on the one they have pierced." ᵇ

The Burial of Jesus

³⁸Later, Joseph of Arimathea asked Pilate for the body of Jesus. Now Joseph was a disciple of Jesus, but secretly because he feared the Jews. With Pilate's permission, he came and took the body away. ³⁹He was accompanied by Nicodemus, the man who earlier had visited Jesus at night. Nicodemus brought a mixture of myrrh and aloes, about seventy-five pounds. ᶜ ⁴⁰Taking Jesus' body, the two of them wrapped it, with the spices, in strips of linen. This was in accordance with Jewish burial customs. ⁴¹At the place where Jesus was crucified, there was a garden, and in the garden a new tomb, in which no one had ever been laid. ⁴²Because it was the Jewish day of Preparation and since the tomb was nearby, they laid Jesus there.

The Empty Tomb

20 Early on the first day of the week, while it was still dark, Mary Magdalene went to the tomb and saw that the stone had been removed from the entrance. ²So she came running to Simon Peter and the other disciple, the one Jesus loved, and said, "They have taken the Lord out of the tomb, and we don't know where they have put him!"

³So Peter and the other disciple started for the tomb. ⁴Both were running, but the other disciple outran Peter and reached the tomb first. ⁵He bent over and looked in at the strips of linen

ª36 Exodus 12:46; Num. 9:12; Psalm 34:20   ᵇ37 Zech. 12:10
ᶜ39 Greek *a hundred litrai* (about 34 kilograms)

lying there but did not go in. 6Then Simon Peter, who was behind him, arrived and went into the tomb. He saw the strips of linen lying there, 7as well as the burial cloth that had been around Jesus' head. The cloth was folded up by itself, separate from the linen. 8Finally the other disciple, who had reached the tomb first, also went inside. He saw and believed. 9(They still did not understand from Scripture that Jesus had to rise from the dead.)

Jesus Appears to Mary Magdalene

10Then the disciples went back to their homes, 11but Mary stood outside the tomb crying. As she wept, she bent over to look into the tomb 12and saw two angels in white, seated where Jesus' body had been, one at the head and the other at the foot.

13They asked her, "Woman, why are you crying?"

"They have taken my Lord away," she said, "and I don't know where they have put him." 14At this, she turned around and saw Jesus standing there, but she did not realize that it was Jesus.

15"Woman," he said, "why are you crying? Who is it you are looking for?"

Thinking he was the gardener, she said, "Sir, if you have carried him away, tell me where you have put him, and I will get him."

16Jesus said to her, "Mary."

She turned toward him and cried out in Aramaic, "Rabboni!" (which means Teacher).

17Jesus said, "Do not hold on to me, for I have not yet returned to the Father. Go instead to my brothers and tell them, 'I am returning to my Father and your Father, to my God and your God.'"

18Mary Magdalene went to the disciples with the news: "I have seen the Lord!" And she told them that he had said these things to her.

Jesus Appears to His Disciples

19On the evening of that first day of the week, when the disciples were together, with the doors locked for fear of the Jews, Jesus came and stood among them and said, "Peace be with you!" 20After he said this, he showed them his hands and side. The disciples were overjoyed when they saw the Lord.

21Again Jesus said, "Peace be with you! As the Father has sent me, I am sending you." 22And with that he breathed on them and said, "Receive the Holy Spirit. 23If you forgive anyone his sins, they are forgiven; if you do not forgive them, they are not forgiven."

Jesus Appears to Thomas

²⁴Now Thomas (called Didymus), one of the Twelve, was not with the disciples when Jesus came. ²⁵So the other disciples told him, "We have seen the Lord!"

But he said to them, "Unless I see the nail marks in his hands and put my finger where the nails were, and put my hand into his side, I will not believe it."

²⁶A week later his disciples were in the house again, and Thomas was with them. Though the doors were locked, Jesus came and stood among them and said, "Peace be with you!" ²⁷Then he said to Thomas, "Put your finger here; see my hands. Reach out your hand and put it into my side. Stop doubting and believe."

²⁸Thomas said to him, "My Lord and my God!"

²⁹Then Jesus told him, "Because you have seen me, you have believed; blessed are those who have not seen and yet have believed."

³⁰Jesus did many other miraculous signs in the presence of his disciples, which are not recorded in this book. ³¹But these are written that you may [a] believe that Jesus is the Christ, the Son of God, and that by believing you may have life in his name.

Jesus and the Miraculous Catch of Fish

21 Afterward Jesus appeared again to his disciples, by the Sea of Tiberias. [b] It happened this way: ²Simon Peter, Thomas (called Didymus), Nathanael from Cana in Galilee, the sons of Zebedee, and two other disciples were together. ³"I'm going out to fish," Simon Peter told them, and they said, "We'll go with you." So they went out and got into the boat, but that night they caught nothing.

⁴Early in the morning, Jesus stood on the shore, but the disciples did not realize that it was Jesus.

⁵He called out to them, "Friends, haven't you any fish?"

"No," they answered.

⁶He said, "Throw your net on the right side of the boat and you will find some." When they did, they were unable to haul the net in because of the large number of fish.

⁷Then the disciple whom Jesus loved said to Peter, "It is the

---

^a31 Some manuscripts *may continue to*   ^b1 That is, Sea of Galilee

Lord!" As soon as Simon Peter heard him say, "It is the Lord," he wrapped his outer garment around him (for he had taken it off) and jumped into the water. 8The other disciples followed in the boat, towing the net full of fish, for they were not far from shore, about a hundred yards. *a* 9When they landed, they saw a fire of burning coals there with fish on it, and some bread. 10Jesus said to them, "Bring some of the fish you have just caught."

11Simon Peter climbed aboard and dragged the net ashore. It was full of large fish, 153, but even with so many the net was not torn. 12Jesus said to them, "Come and have breakfast." None of the disciples dared ask him, "Who are you?" They knew it was the Lord. 13Jesus came, took the bread and gave it to them, and did the same with the fish. 14This was now the third time Jesus appeared to his disciples after he was raised from the dead.

Jesus Reinstates Peter

15When they had finished eating, Jesus said to Simon Peter, "Simon son of John, do you truly love me more than these?"

"Yes, Lord," he said, "you know that I love you."

Jesus said, "Feed my lambs."

16Again Jesus said, "Simon son of John, do you truly love me?"

He answered, "Yes, Lord, you know that I love you."

Jesus said, "Take care of my sheep."

17The third time he said to him, "Simon son of John, do you love me?"

Peter was hurt because Jesus asked him the third time, "Do you love me?" He said, "Lord, you know all things; you know that I love you."

Jesus said, "Feed my sheep. 18I tell you the truth, when you were younger you dressed yourself and went where you wanted; but when you are old you will stretch out your hands, and someone else will dress you and lead you where you do not want to go." 19Jesus said this to indicate the kind of death by which Peter would glorify God. Then he said to him, "Follow me!"

20Peter turned and saw that the disciple whom Jesus loved was following them. (This was the one who had leaned back against Jesus at the supper and had said, "Lord, who is going

a8 Greek about two hundred cubits (about 90 meters)

to betray you?'') ²¹When Peter saw him, he asked, ''Lord, what about him?''

²²Jesus answered, ''If I want him to remain alive until I return, what is that to you? You must follow me.'' ²³Because of this, the rumor spread among the brothers that this disciple would not die. But Jesus did not say that he would not die; he only said, ''If I want him to remain alive until I return, what is that to you?''

²⁴This is the disciple who testifies to these things and who wrote them down. We know that his testimony is true.

²⁵Jesus did many other things as well. If every one of them were written down, I suppose that even the whole world would not have room for the books that would be written.

PART THREE

Other Helps for Beginning Again

PROPHECIES FULFILLED

Prophecy	Fulfillment
Genesis 3:15	1 John 3:8
Genesis 12:3	Matthew 1:1 & Galatians 3:8,16
Genesis 17:19 & Genesis 21:2	Luke 3:23-34 & Romans 4:18-20
Genesis 49:10	Luke 3:33 & Matthew 25:31,32
Daniel 9:25	Galatians 4:4
Isaiah 9:1,2	Matthew 4:13-16
Isaiah 9:6,7	Luke 1:32,33
Micah 5:2	Luke 2:4-7
Numbers 24:17,19	Matthew 1:1,2 & Revelation 22:16 & 2 Peter 1:19
Isaiah 7:14	Luke 1:26-35 & Matthew 1:21-23
Jeremiah 31:15	Matthew 2:16-18
Hosea 11:1	Matthew 2:14,15
Psalm 45:6,7 & Psalm 102:25-27	Hebrews 1:8-12
Isaiah 40:3-5	Luke 3:2-4
Isaiah 61:1,2	Luke 4:18,19,21

Psalm 78:2-4	Matthew 13:34,35
Deuteronomy 18:15	Acts 3:20-22
Psalm 110:4	Hebrews 5:5,6
Zechariah 9:9	Mark 11:7,9,11
Psalm 8:2	Matthew 21:15,16
Malachi 3:1 & Psalm 69:9	John 2:12-17
Psalm 41:9	John 13:18
Isaiah 53:5,7,9,12	Mark 10:45;15:4,5, 27,28 & Matthew 27:57,60
Isaiah 50:6 & Zechariah 12:10	Matthew 26:67; 27:26 & John 20:27
Isaiah 53:1-4	John 1:10,11;12:37, 38 & Matthew 8:16,17
Psalm 16:10	Acts 2:25-32
Psalm 2:7	Acts 13:33
Psalm 68:18	Ephesians 4:8

DO YOU HAVE A CHURCH HOME?

If you are a new Christian, or if you are rededicating your life to Him and you don't have a church in which to worship, the Referral Department staff of Coral Ridge Ministries would like to assist you.

The referral system of Coral Ridge Ministries has a membership list of churches nationwide which have expressed an interest in welcoming Christians into their congregations for fellowship, growth and service to the Lord.

Simply fill out the form below and mail it to Coral Ridge Ministries, P.O. Box 40, Ft. Lauderdale, Florida 33302, and we will see if there is a member church in your area. If so, we will correspond with you and give you that information. You are never under obligation to join.

In the meantime, the next page has some tips on how to find a solid Christ-centered church in which you can grow strong in your faith.

CUT HERE

Name _____ Phone _____

Address _____ Apt # _____

City _____ State _____ Zip _____

HOW TO CHOOSE A CHURCH

When looking for a local church, we would recommend that you look for the following characteristics:

1. Doctrinal Purity — A church should hold to the essential doctrines of the Christian faith, such as the Trinity, the incarnation of Christ, the substitutionary death of Christ to pay for our sins, the bodily resurrection of Christ from the grave, the personhood and deity of the Holy Spirit, and the total depravity of mankind. A church must teach that salvation is through faith in the Lord and Savior Jesus Christ alone. The Bible must be accepted as the authoritative, inspired and infallible Word of God.

2. Spiritual Vitality — A church should be a group of people who worship God in "spirit and in truth." There should be a real concern for God and for His Kingdom. The faith of the leaders and of the congregation should not only be an intellectual acceptance of Christian truths, but a sincere faith which influences their lives.

3. Community of Love — Christ taught that the Church should have a special love between each and every member of the congregation. Churches which have inner frictions, open outbursts of anger, and a lack of forgivenesss should be avoided. Christ's disciples are commanded to love each other and to sacrifice in order to meet each other's needs, both spiritual and physical.

4. Center of Service — A church should have a number of ministries organized which will allow each individual member to have an opportunity for service. These ministries should include the areas of evangelism, education and social outreach.

*****

We trust that these guidelines will help you decide which church in your area best fits the Biblical ideal. However, none of them will be perfect; therefore, you should pray earnestly about your choice and choose the local church which is, in your estimate, the best.

Once you have joined a church, you need to work within it to make it even better. Just as there are no perfect Christians until Christ returns, there are no perfect churches. Therefore, be realistic about your evaluation of the churches in your area and choose one in which you will be able to grow spiritually and serve Christ.

ANSWER KEY

CHAPTER ONE

1. They knew they had been forgiven for their sins and were going to Heaven.

2. This was a message which could really help people in their relationship with God.

3. Yes; by believing in Jesus Christ as our personal Lord and Savior.

4. 1 John 5:13; John 3:14; Ephesians 2:8,9.

CHAPTER TWO

1. To walk each day in faith, confessing our sins, turning away from evil, and turning to Jesus for forgiveness, grace, and strength.

2. When they begin to base their daily walk with God on their works rather than faith in God's grace in Jesus Christ.

3. He should stop depending on his good works, confess his sins, and begin walking by faith.

4. The death of Christ for our sins and the daily intercession of Jesus for us.

5. Yes; whenever we allow ourselves to disobey Christ in thought, word, or deed, we have allowed our old self to control us and have failed to walk by faith.

6. By recognizing sinful tendencies early, confessing them at once, repenting immediately, and asking God to forgive our sins and help us to obey Christ.

CHAPTER THREE

1. What it teaches about itself and how we can study it effectively.

2. Yes; 2 Timothy 3:16,17.

3. All the parts of the Bible are inspired by God; the Bible is true in all that it teaches.

4. The ultimate source of the Bible is God Himself.

5. Reading, observation, notetaking and interpretation.

6. Use the Bible as its own interpreter. Use the immediate context to clarify the passage. Study all of Scripture on the subject the passage speaks about. Apply the teaching in your daily life.

CHAPTER FOUR

1. Cast our burdens on Him in prayer.

2. Confession, thanksgiving, petition, intercession and adoration.

3. Right relationship with God, right relationship with people, repentance and believing according to God's will.

CHAPTER FIVE

1. Fellowship.

2. Christian fellowship is based on the common union all believers have with Christ.

3. No; for the fellowship God calls us to is one which is "in the light" and not one filled with hypocrisy and unconfessed sins.

CHAPTER SIX

1. Because the Church is God's people directly involved in preaching His Gospel, making disciples, and praying for His will to be done on earth.

2. Regardless of how perfectly we organize society, little real improvement will take place until people themselves have been transformed by Christ to desire good rather than evil.

3. Believers were to preserve and add flavor to life.

4. Jesus taught a few men who reached others. This is how it should be done today.

CHAPTER SEVEN

1. Grace, Man, God, Christ, Faith.

2. **Grace**

    a. Heaven is a free gift.
    b. It is not earned or deserved.

    Man

    a. Is a sinner.
    b. Cannot save himself.

    God

    a. Is merciful.
    b. Is just.

Christt

a.   Who He is—the infinite eternal God-man.
b.   What He did—died on the cross and rose from the dead to purchase a place for us in Heaven.

Faith

a.   What it is: trusting only in Jesus Christ as Lord and Savior.
b.   What it is not: intellectual assent or temporal faith.

3.   Romans 6:23; Ephesians 2:8,9; Romans 3:23; Romans 3:20; Titus 3:5; Jeremiah 31:3; Habakkuk 1:13; Exodus 34:7; John 1:1,14; Romans 3:21-26; 2 Corinthians 5:21; Acts 16:31; James 2:19

4.   (a)   Have you came to a place in your spiritual life where you know for certain that if you were to die you would go to Heaven?
     (b)   Suppose that you were to die today and stand before God and He were to say to you, "Why should I let you into my Heaven?" What would you say?

*****

FOR FURTHER STUDY*

1. Cosgrove, Jr., Francis M. Essentials of New Life. Colorado Springs, CO: Navpress, 1978. (A ministry of The Navigators)

2. Home Bible studies are offered by Coral Ridge Ministries. If you would like to continue your study of the Scriptures, just write to Dr. Kennedy at P.O. Box 40, Ft. Lauderdale, FL 33302 and ask to receive the Home Bible study course. You should receive your first booklet in four to six weeks.

3. Kennedy, Dr. D. James. Why I Believe. Waco, TX: Word Publishing Co., 1980. (Can be ordered from Coral Ridge Ministries.)

4. Sproul, R.C. Knowing Scripture. Downers Grove, IL: InterVarsity Press, 1977.

5. Stott, John R. Baptism and Fullness: The Work of the Holy Spirit Today. Downers Grove, IL: InterVarsity Press, 1976.

6. Stott, John R. Basic Christianity. Downers Grove, IL: InterVarsity Press, 1982.

7. Stott, John R. Men Made New. Downers Grove, IL: InterVarsity Press, 1977.

8. Stott, John R. Our Guilty Silence. Grand Rapids, MI: William B. Eerdmans Publishing Company, 1974.

9. Stott, John R. Your Mind Matters. Downers Grove, IL: InterVarsity Press, 1972.

*With the exception of Why I Believe (#3 above), these books are *not* available from Coral Ridge Ministries.

IMPORTANT BIBLE VERSES (NIV)

Salvation — John 3:16

"For God so loved the world that he gave his one and only Son, that whoever believes in him shall not perish but have eternal life."

Victory Over Temptation — 1 Corinthians 10:13

"No temptation has seized you except what is common to man. And God is faithful; he will not let you be tempted beyond what you can bear. But when you are tempted . . . he will also provide a way out so that you can stand up under it."

Forgiveness — 1 John 1:9

"If we confess our sins, he is faithful and just and will forgive us our sins and purify us from all unrighteousness."

Asking in Faith — James 1:5,6

"If any of you lacks wisdom, he should ask God, who gives generously to all without finding fault, and it will be given to him. But when he asks, he must believe and not doubt, because he who doubts is like a wave of the sea, blown and tossed by the wind."

Promise of His Presence — Hebrews 13:5

". . . Never will I leave you; never will I forsake you."

Victory Through His Word — Psalm 119:9,11

"How can a young man keep his way pure? By living according to your word . . ."

"I have hidden your word in my heart that I might not sin against you."

Confidence Through Prayer — 1 John 5:14,15

"This is the confidence we have in approaching God: that if we ask anything according to his will he hears us."

Applying His Word — Joshua 1:8

"Do not let this Book of the Law depart from your mouth; meditate on it day and night, so that you may be careful to do everything written in it. Then you will be prosperous and successful."

Successfully Witnessing for Christ — Acts 1:8

"But you will receive power when the Holy Spirit comes on you; and you will be my witnesses in Jerusalem, and in all Judea and Samaria, and to the ends of the earth."

Peace and Assurance Through Prayer — Philippians 4:6,7

"Do not be anxious about anything, but in everything, by prayer and petition, with thanksgiving, present your requests to God. And the peace of God, which transcends all understanding will guard your hearts and your minds in Christ Jesus."

Promise of Answered Prayer — John 16:23,24

"I tell you the truth, my Father will give you whatever you ask in my name . . . Ask and you will receive, and your joy will be complete."

Successfully Winning Souls — Matthew 4:19

"Come, follow me . . . and I will make you fishers of men."

NOTES

NOTES